Cognitive Harmony

An Adventure in Mental Fitness

Jerry Stocking

For more information
on Cognitive Harmony Seminars, Tapes and Books,
see page 199.

Editor: Jackie Stocking
Copy Editor: Roger Anderson
Proofreaders: Judy Bates, Claire Blehr, Mike Dowd, Wayne Furnweger,
        John Patrick Gill, Kate Marrs, Chas Stevens
Cover Design: Jerry Stocking
Illustrations: Jerry Stocking

Thank-you to everyone who aided in the production of this book.

A special thank-you to Karen Bates for playing with Molly while my wife and
I attended to the creation of this book.

Published by
Moose Ear Press
First Printing 1991

ISBN: 0-9629593-0-8

Table of Contents

Index of Illustrations

This book is dedicated to my grandmother, Twinkle. While in her nineties, she was still looking on the bright side of life and lighting up the lives of the people around her.

This book is also dedicated to all of the people who have done and will do Courses and Seminars in Cognitive Harmony. Thank-you for your willingness to play and for the contributions you have made and will make to humanity.

Preface

Let's say that you are from Mars and have just arrived on Earth. You have been transported from your planet into a little room in a little house. There is a chess set in the room, and your job is to understand what it is. You could, if you are of a scientific orientation, break the pieces down by figuring out their molecular structure. You could note the exact size and location of each piece. Then you could analyze the table: its height, width, material, shape, color, texture, mass, weight, and other features.

Unless you saw the process of the game by observing two people playing chess, the significance of the chess set would elude you. Generally, what I have found in this culture is that people spend time on the content of their lives and ignore the process, the game itself. I'm not saying this is bad, but I am offering an alternative called *paying attention to the process or the dance of life*. Attending to process results in observing the flow and the game of life.

This book is not very characteristic of our culture. In the United States of America today, the majority of interactions between people deal with content. Our focus is typified with such questions as, "What do you do? How much money do you make? How many kids do you have? What do you drive? Where do you live? How long have you done it? How long are you going to do it?" We spend most of our time busily moving content around and acting like "human-doings" rather than "human-beings." Culture's attention (our attention) is constantly on the "stuff" of life—content. It seems as though culture is no more than the content, or data, that is entered into a computer. However, it is possible to pay attention to the "dance" of life—process. Staying with the above computer analogy, we may think of process as the software that influences and controls content.

This book will sweep you up from the world of content and place you into the world of process. I will describe the differences between content and process and give you exercises which will enable you to discover yourself at the level of process. From that point you will be able to participate in life observing and relating to the processes that go on with people rather than viewing them only in terms of content.

In life there is a lot of content to keep you busy. When you attend to content, you must work on every piece of it individually; this effort can easily keep you *busy* for your lifetime. There are, however, a limited number of processes which completely influence the content.

Content is like the basic chemicals of life, and process is the way they are noticed, combined, mixed and changed. Process changes the very nature and content of life.

Process is not as easy to observe as content, primarily because most people are unfamiliar with process and unskilled in noticing it or paying attention to its flow. But, with practice, you will become competent at process. You will be able to influence all aspects of your life and dance in the wonder, mystery and adventure of life.

My promise to you is that when you read this book and complete each exercise, you will be able to experience life at the level of process. Doing so will allow you a new degree of control and influence over your life that few people ever know. You will live with harmony and will move from being a pawn to being the player who moves the pieces. Interested? Read on and do the exercises.

People are mysteries to themselves. This is not surprising since most people keep themselves quite busy in the pursuit of results: results intended to prove their competence where it isn't, outside themselves. As people discover themselves, by turning inward and observing process, they discover that they are already competent and that their job in life is to allow this competence to flow to all aspects of life. If you are busy trying to prove that you are a good dancer, you will probably miss the joy and delight of the dance. Given a chance, your natural competence will allow you to dance elegantly and effortlessly with life.

· · · ·

To get the most from this book, you will need to set your current beliefs and attitudes to the side. Please do the following exercise:

Close your eyes and get comfortable; take several deep relaxed breaths. Now imagine a safe. Your safe can be made from wood or metal or any material you wish, and it can be anywhere that you choose. The safe is one in which you can put your belief systems and attitudes. I request that you imagine yourself putting your belief systems into your safe. I wouldn't want you to go anywhere without them, so make sure that when you are through reading, you go to your safe and take your beliefs out again. But please make sure to put them away when you continue reading.

You have had your particular set of beliefs around long enough that it may seem a little strange to put them into a safe, but please do so anyway. I promise not to tamper with them, and I doubt that anybody else wants them, so they are safe there. When you have put your beliefs away, continue reading. Thank-you.

•   •   •   •

I have discovered that when people are learning something new, it is often useful for them not to filter it through their current set of beliefs. Beliefs work as filters; beliefs filter experience. By setting the filters to the side, people can learn rapidly and easily. If you have a question as you are reading, ask yourself if your question was generated from your beliefs. If so, put those beliefs into the safe, too, so that you can process the material faster and more easily.

When we were children, everything was new to us. We observed everything that went on in our childhood world and learned rapidly from it. As we grew older, we needed to make sense of the world and did so by forming concepts which, if reinforced often enough, became beliefs.

There is nothing wrong with beliefs. There is, however, a tendency for us to put the cart in front of the horse and allow beliefs to influence our perceptions. This is a dangerous pattern because it leads us into the habit of replacing information we could be learning from the world with information constructed and filtered by us. As a result of having this habit, we miss what is really present and live in an unreal world.

When we attempt to distinguish between that which is truly there and that which we have created, we are less likely to miss the real world. It may be useful to think of information as "in-formation": material which is not yet fully formed, but is in the process of being formed.

Introduction

"Like water to the fish, air to the bird and man to himself."

Anonymous

$\mathcal{F}$or years humankind has been attempting to discover what makes people behave the way they do. How is it possible that when confronted with the same task or problem, two people will attempt very different means of solving it? Why do some people continually excel while others perform at a mediocre level? Over the years, scientists and philosophers have attempted to explain these phenomena, and some of their explanations even sound plausible. What has been missing is the ability to consistently alter and improve individual performance in any given field. Also missing is the ability to discern specifically what one person is doing well and pass these skills on behaviorally to another person.

We are faced with an opportunity today that I find exciting, scary and tremendously valuable. I perceive that we are closer as a race to gaining some control and even mastery over our behaviors. Imagine the benefits of such an advance! Mastery allows us to get on to much more important areas of development.

Mastery over our behaviors will be more important and far reaching than such momentous developments as the invention of the telephone or the automobile. Imagine for a moment that you are in a world with cars (like our world today), but nobody in this world knows how to drive them. The inhabitants don't even know with any consistency what makes cars go forward or backward. Cars are fairly simple. They can move forward or backward or remain in one place. It takes relatively simple actions to make a car perform any of these three functions. However, people are a good deal more complex than cars, so it is little wonder that we don't know, with any consistency, what makes us work.

A person uses 159 muscles to lift his arm three inches off his thigh. Go ahead and try it: put your arm on your thigh and then lift it approximately three inches. It's pretty easy to coordinate 159 muscles isn't it? Now congratulate yourself for your cleverness and coordination at having accomplished such a feat.

We have at our disposal, right now, the capacity to determine behaviorally what makes us tick: how to excel, how to communicate at deep and effective levels, how to motivate ourselves to produce just what we choose and how to be totally satisfied and happy regardless of what we produce. One difficulty we face is that the new methodology that makes all of this possible is too simple. It does not require understanding, deep thinking, philosophy or science. However, the new methodology does require that people observe themselves as a creative essence with unique and wonderful qualities to be noticed and appreciated and that people see themselves from other than their human and cultural perspective. Imagine for a moment explaining what water is to a fish. It would probably be a very difficult task since the fish has never known anything but water. It is a similar task to talk to people about themselves. We are inside ourselves and know everything only from that perspective. This perspective is created by culture and our personal belief structures.

·   ·   ·   ·

In the Genesis creation story, God created the world in seven days. It seems likely that by the eighth day, humankind was already second guessing God's creation of the world by figuring out how it should be different or how it could have been done better. Imagine creating something as spectacular as the world and then being criticized for it. Finally God had enough of the criticism and gathered together three "wise men" to figure out how to get away from people. One "wise man" suggested that God could go to the tallest mountain and hide there. God wouldn't hide there because it would not be long before people would climb the tallest mountain. Another "wise man" suggested that God hide on the moon; surely nobody would bother going to the moon. God knew that would not do either since, before long, people would go to the moon. The third "wise man" said, "I have a place where you can be safe and avoid the criticism and complaints of everybody. Hide in people themselves. They will never look there, and if they do, they will be people of such accomplishment that you will not mind being discovered." God knew that to be true and hid inside each person.

•   •   •   •

To have a dialogue with a human being about himself, I have discovered that direct conversation alone is not sufficient. To discover this for yourself, think back for a moment to all the times that you said you would do something and then didn't do it. Think of all the times that you said you would never do something again and then did that very thing. Think of all the times you knew that something would be bad for you or lead to negative consequences and you went ahead and did it anyway, even though you knew better.

I have found some ways to effectively talk to a person about himself, the most direct being through simple exercises that result in a level of discovery. This book is a collection of informative material, stories, pictures and exercises. The exercises have been proven effective by thousands of people who have taken part in workshops with me and then practiced the elements of Cognitive Harmony which are illustrated throughout this book. (Cognitive Harmony, which is a methodology that I've created, is the process of relating effectively to yourself and other people; increasing your enjoyment and awareness of every moment of your life.) The purpose of this book is to provide you with the tools necessary for you to have exactly what you want in any aspect of your life. If you want turmoil, that is what you will have. If you want bliss, you will have bliss.

A word of warning: "This Book Works!" I don't recommend that you use this book unless you are ready for more satisfaction and delight than you now have in your life. The methodology in this book is quite simple. It does not require prior education or any particular training or abilities. Instead, it uses abilities that you already have and are either ignoring or not using.

A second word of warning: "This Book is Simple!" I invite you to set aside your daily complexities while you are living this book. I say "living this book" because reading it is not sufficient. Integrating it into your life will contribute to the quality of your life as a whole. So please, read the book and conscientiously do the exercises. It won't take a lot of time, and you may find yourself having fun.

Throughout the book I have alternated the use of masculine and feminine pronouns in an attempt to show no preference for either sex. The use of these pronouns is random, and I suggest that you fill in your own gender preference.

I make no claims as to the accuracy of anything presented in this book. To claim accuracy is to claim a correlation with reality. I have little idea of what reality is and even less certainty that if there is such a thing as reality I would recognize it.

I do claim that what is presented in this book is **useful**. This claim is based on my personal experience with thousands of people who have taken part in my seminars over many years. I have watched people and received reports from people as their lives changed after brief contact with Cognitive Harmony. People's lives get easier, more enjoyable, more fun and more successful as they adventure in mental fitness applying the tools of Cognitive Harmony.

Evidence for most of what is said in this book can be discovered through doing the exercises. I have found that in the domain of awareness evidence discovered personally is often more convincing and useful than evidence cited from an external source. For this reason, I have included very little evidence in this book. This lack of evidence is not because I don't have the evidence, but because I don't want to hamper your ability to discover it yourself through observation and doing the exercises.

1
The Story

*T*o make the journey a little easier, let's start somewhere near the beginning. In the beginning there is nothing, and from nothing everything is **possible**. From nothing we will start with a room which is dark and has none of the ordinary distinctions that we rely on to make sense of the world.

The Room

Let's imagine that you find yourself alone and in the dark with no reference to ever having been anywhere before. There is no light and no way to tell where you are. It is impossible to make sense of where you are without comparing it to other places you have been. The room is completely dark and silent. It is not possible to discern exactly what size it is, and it may not even be of a constant size. One thing you do know is here you are in this room. You think.

If you are philosophical, one of the first questions you might ask yourself is how you even know the room is here. Or you might ask why you are here or how you got here. None of these questions sheds much light on your situation although asking them does pass some time. The questions and possible answers do not help your immediate situation. Since it is dark and silent, you cannot rely on your sight or hearing to make sense of the room. For now you just call it a room; it seems a bit easier to call it something so that you have a way to refer to your new surroundings. You are willing to allow for the possibility of being inaccurate because naming it a room provides you with the comfort of having some point of reference.

There are a few important aspects of this place you notice right from the start. One of these is that the room is cloaked in complete darkness. But you are in luck. There are two different ways that you can determine what is in the room. You have a flashlight that will last for a long time, and you have the ability to **trust** yourself. Your flashlight has a narrow beam and allows you to see only very small parts of the room at any point in time. The beam is so narrow that it is sometimes difficult to direct it right where you want it. You can only use this flashlight for a number of hours and then you must recharge it, which requires turning it off.

The second way of knowing what is in the room is to simply trust that you know what is here. This type of knowing is not like the flashlight in that it seems much less tangible. All-encompassing trust is more uncomfortable than one little point of certainty, which the flashlight provides within a very limited context. Knowing by way of trust allows complete knowing of everything. To trust seems opposed to reason and logic, and the more you depend on your flashlight the more difficult this second way of knowing becomes.

There are two types of rules in this room: those which can be broken and those which cannot. Rules that can be broken are those made up by you or others in the room. Rules that cannot be broken are those that are imposed by the room. It is often hard to distinguish between the two types of rules, and the more time you spend in the room, the less clear the difference between the two becomes. This creates an element of danger for you since the consequences for breaking one type of rule are very different from the consequences for breaking the other. Breaking a rule that can be broken affects the quality of your life. If you break a rule that cannot be broken, you must leave the room.

This brings us to one of the major problems with the room: "Nothing is what it seems to be." How the room seems to us depends on our perspective: which is limited, and the room may not be limited. At all points we are sure of what we see, but the correlation between what we see and what is here is weak at best.

Here you are in the room. One thing for sure is that you probably won't run around in the dark a lot. Running is not conducive to survival when you have no idea what is around you. So you begin to make up and impose your own rules. The first rule you impose on yourself is that you are interested in your survival. With this rule comes the possibility of death; along with this comes the responsibility of distinguishing what threatens your survival and what doesn't. Mistakes in this area are very costly and may cause you to forfeit your continued presence in the room, which is synonymous with death. Survival is your ultimate goal; all behaviors and future rules must come from this first rule. The second rule is that this may not be a safe place, so you must move slowly while constantly assessing whether or not you are moving slowly and safely enough. This rule allows you to be nagged constantly by the fear of what is ahead and requires frequent use of the flashlight. You soon become so used to the limitation of the beam of the flashlight that you rest while the flashlight is recharging. The flashlight becomes indispensable and you become dependent on the limitation, treating it with a kind of reverence. The flashlight becomes your only link with all that is in the room. You ignore your ability to **trust** while you focus on the flashlight. You may even begin to think that the flashlight is the only way there is of knowing or observing.

As you explore the room, you discover all manner of wonderful people and wonderful things. There are some aspects of the room that you like and some that you don't. You go about your process of discovery and find that the room is even bigger than you can imagine. Your little flashlight sometimes seems insufficient for the purpose of exploration and you may begin to ponder why the room is so big and your flashlight so small. Why are you in the room anyway? What is the point?

You meet people from time to time who also have flashlights and curiosity similar to yours. Some of these people have been in the room longer than you and some have just arrived. Usually the people that have just arrived are enthusiastic and curious, and they never tire in their explorations. The ones that have been here longer have already come up with answers about why they are in the room. Some of these people will even keep their flashlights focused on very small areas and attempt to keep themselves in one spot. They can only see you if you get in the way of their flashlights. The longer one of them keeps his beam in one particular place, the more threatening it becomes for him to move it.

There are certain people who find something that they like in the room. This thing makes survival seem a little more certain, or at least, it reduces their fear of never knowing what will come next. They want to make sure that they don't lose this thing they like. They take it with them everywhere. If they meet someone else with a similar object they will be comfortable. Of course, as soon as they **need** to have the object with them, the thought of not having it becomes a threat. Their future explorations are affected by the need to have the object. The object of their affection can be a thing, another person or even an idea. The more tightly they hold this object, the more attention they focus on it and the less they are able to explore their surroundings.

Dependence on the flashlight is easy to develop, but it has some built-in problems. Since the beam is so narrow, you will always have much more of the room in darkness than in view. You may even become fearful of what your beam is not shining on. You may imagine all sorts of awful unilluminated areas. You may also become afraid of the time it takes for the light to recharge.

The easiest way to be secure in this room is to stay within your own little area that you have fully explored. For this strategy to work, it is also necessary to only allow people into your area who are limiting their focus. With a little imagination, you can even decide that your area is really the whole room. You can spend your days focusing your light on familiar objects and people within your area. One problem you will have with this approach is that there will be a nagging realization that your area is not all there is and that this "security" you have developed is not so secure after all. Remember that in this room nothing is what it seems. The sense of security you develop in this room is an illusion and is really insecure.

Then one day, as you are walking along, your foot hits something that was not supposed to be on the floor. You bend over to discover a book that somehow mysteriously appeared in your little space. You focus your flashlight on this book and within you swells a sense of curiosity and exploration that you have longed for. These sensations mount as you read on.

You are now holding the book, <u>Cognitive Harmony</u>, and feeling it in your hands. Discover how the book feels. Determine the weight, texture, smoothness, size and temperature. ... Then examine how the book looks: What color is it? How thick is it? Is there a design on it? Notice the contrast of the type to the rest of the page. Notice the open spaces around the edges of the pages. Observe everything you can visually about the book. ... Now tap the book and listen to the sound. Are you making the sound or is the book? Flip through the pages and listen to the sound. Now stop at any page and read a few sentences out loud. Listen to the sound of your voice. What thoughts do you have about the sound of your voice?

What did you learn from examining the book? ... Is it like any other book you have seen? ... What conclusions can you make from your examination? ... Do you think other people would reach these same conclusions? ... What conclusions or observations might other people make?

Some possible conclusions from your examination are the following:

- That you are a master at coordination.

- That as you pay attention to something, you lose the ability to pay attention to something else. There are a limited number of things that you can pay attention to at any point in time.

- That you are proficient with your senses.

- That you take your senses for granted.

- That other people may perceive the same object differently than you do.

- That to make sense of your perceptions, you label them with language.

- That once you have labeled something, that label influences your next perception of that thing.

- That you influence the viewing of the book, and it is often hard to tell what are attributes of the book and what are attributes of the viewing process.

- That you have a tendency to make judgments on limited information.

These possible conclusions, and much more about how you think and how you make sense of the world, will be discussed throughout the following chapters.

2

To Earth

To make the journey a little easier let's start somewhere near the beginning. In the beginning there is nothing and from nothing everything is **possible**. From nothing we will start with a room which is dark and has none of the ordinary distinctions that we rely on to make sense of the world.

The first thing you want to do in the room is to make some sort of sense as to where you are and what is happening. You make judgments and decisions to better understand your surroundings and to make the unknown more palatable. The accuracy of your judgments will contribute to your likelihood of survival and will also contribute to the quality of your time in the room. If you make an accurate judgment about something you are more likely to use it appropriately and to build reasonable expectations regarding it.

If there is a bear standing behind you, then there really is a bear standing behind you. If you think that there is a bear standing behind you, there may or may not be one. Thinking there is a bear does not *affect the bear much, if there is one, but it does affect you. If you think there is a bear behind you and there is, you have an opportunity to act appropriately. If you think there is a bear behind you and there is not one, you may act inappropriately. If you think there is one too often when in fact there isn't, you will start to have problems. An imagined threat to your survival has the same effect on your body as a real threat.*

The simplest place to read this book is on earth. As I pointed out in the Preface, beliefs tend to influence perception so that we no longer see what is here. With the aid of our belief system, we hear and see what we believe will be here. A system in which beliefs determine perception takes us farther from the earth, as it is, and closer to a world made up by us. Before we move on to observing process, we will distinguish between the content that is real and that which is a product of our beliefs. To do this, we will focus on learning the difference between grounded observations and ungrounded observations.

Stop reading and observe your surroundings. Look around the room . . . look at yourself . . . look at the other people in the room (if there are other people in the room). Make observations and write them down.

Here is a brief list of observations created during a workshop. We could create millions of other lists because, in life, we make observations constantly.

We are interested.
His foot moved.
She is uptight.
His hands are touching.
There are five men and seven women in the room.
Everybody is nervous.
Several people are smiling.
She is smiling and giggling.
He is apprehensive.
They are sitting in open postures.
She is skeptical.
The people in the room are relaxing more.
He had on casual clothes.
Her legs were crossed.

Some observations are obvious while some are unspoken and unnoticed. To determine which observations are grounded (that is, to return you to noticing what is here on earth), imagine that we have twelve randomly-picked jurors who looked at the same things you did. How many of the observations you wrote down would all twelve jurors be able to observe and agree with? Would all twelve jurors agree that the people were interested? No. "Interested" is an interpretation and is not observable. The jurors would be able to observe that the people were sitting and facing toward the front of the room with their eyes open and looking in the direction of the speaker and that no one was yawning.

Grounded observations: Sensory-based observations that twelve randomly picked jurors would agree are true.

The following are examples of grounded assessments: *He is wearing a blue shirt. There are twelve people in this room. She was sitting on a chair. He bought a car.*

Ungrounded observations: Subjective interpretations not based on sensory data.

Examples of ungrounded assessments are: *He is wearing a nice blue shirt. All of the people were interested. She was smiling. He was happy because he just bought a good car.*

Each person must make his own determination regarding what he has observed. For instance, instead of "interested," a juror could interpret what he has observed as a room full of people meditating, or deep in thought, or afraid to look away because they might miss something. How do you determine that someone is interested? You can observe behaviors, but the interpretation "interested" is one that you add to your observation. You can never really know whether people are interested in something; you can only label them as such. This label and lack of sensory evidence makes "interested" an ungrounded observation.

If policemen have five eyewitnesses to an accident, they usually get five very different reports. I read a study about a group of thirty people who were shown a film of a car accident and then were given a questionnaire to complete. One of the questions asked whether the accident happened in front of or behind the yield sign. Fifteen people said it happened in front of and

Returning To Earth

**Thoughts
and Language**

Think	Yes
Like	Maybe
Should	No
Could	Look
Will	Say
Hello	Did

The Senses

Sounds

Pictures

Feelings

The Earth

Illustration: Returning to Earth

fifteen people said it happened behind, when in fact there was no yield sign in the film. But all of the participants imagined that they saw a sign when they were asked the question.

Imagine how useful it would be to know whether you were observing something real (grounded) or judging something based on your opinions (ungrounded). You would know what you were adding and what was there and could react to real bears instead of unreal bears. You could be guided by "what is" in a particular situation rather than "what you think is." Grounded observation isn't better than ungrounded, but simply knowing the difference between the two would contribute to distinguishing between what is sensory-based and what you have created with pictures and sounds internally.

Here are explanations of my previous examples of grounded and ungrounded observations.

His hands are touching. Twelve jurors would be able to observe hands touching, so it is a grounded assessment.

Several people are smiling. Smiling is an interpretation which implies some intent or a specific disposition, so it is an ungrounded assessment. To some jurors it might be a smile; to others it could be a grimace. "The sides of their mouths moved upward" is a grounded assessment.

We can all agree that something is blue. We could go beyond that and argue that it is not, but I'm not sure how fruitful that would be in our pursuit of clarity. Grounded assessments contribute to your ability to observe; ungrounded assessments contribute to your ability to judge and evaluate.

They are sitting in open postures. This is an ungrounded assessment. "Sitting" is grounded; "open" implies some intent or disposition in the person, so it is ungrounded.

He had on casual clothes. Casual clothes is an ungrounded assessment. It depends on the jurors' definition of the term. What are casual clothes to one person might be sloppy or even dress clothes to another. Not everyone has your identical definition of casual. Perhaps they should (ungrounded), but I don't think that they do.

She is skeptical. Skeptical is an ungrounded assessment. What does a person look like when she is skeptical? What is her body position? What expression does she have on her face? The concept of "skeptical" is dependent upon the observer and thus is an ungrounded assessment.

Her legs were crossed. Grounded.

His foot moved. Grounded.

Everybody is nervous. Nervousness, stress, and tension are not sensory-based judgments, they are ungrounded assessments. They exist only when someone is around to label them.

He is apprehensive. Ungrounded.

The people in the room are relaxing more. Ungrounded.

She is uptight. Ungrounded.

There are five men and seven women in the room. Grounded.

She is smiling and giggling. Ungrounded.

One way to have your ungrounded assessments be more useful is to qualify them. Get in the habit of stating grounded observations as fact and stating ungrounded observations as opinions. Beginning opinions with phrases such as, "seems like," "in my opinion," "suppose that," "probably," and "perhaps" allows people to hear what you are saying as your opinion rather than as fact. Qualifying will *usually* have you gain credibility with others and with yourself. It *might* make life easier.

While working with some school administrators, I was surprised to discover that they could not make grounded assessments. They get paid for their ungrounded assessments like, "This kid is a little slow," "This child is very bright," "This boy is a trouble maker," or "This girl is a great student." Not only did the school administrators have difficulty making grounded statements, they couldn't see any value in making them. They had only been rewarded for making ungrounded observations. They brought in the "this is good—this is not so good" perspective without having had the alternative to make grounded assessments.

When people put themselves into a position of being the judge and the jury, as the school administrators had done, they can make ungrounded statements as though they are grounded statements or vice versa. This type of thinking leads to our missing what is real and thinking that judgments and opinions really are true. The most effective way to deal with or teach another person is to start from a shared reality of grounded assessments.

How much of your everyday conversation is grounded and how much of it is ungrounded? How much of what you say in a day is sensory-based? Remember, if you say "Good morning" to someone, that is not sensory-based. The "good" is a judgment made up by you.

I've noticed that people have fewer problems when they make grounded assessments than when they make ungrounded assessments. The word *problem* itself is an ungrounded assessment. *Suffering* is another ungrounded assessment. So, without ungrounded assessments there would be no suffering. In the realm of sensory-based observations, you may have pain, but you won't have the regrets and remorse and all of the "would-have's," "could-have's," and "should-have's" that live in the world of ungrounded assessments. Your judgments and opinions influence the quality of your life. If you think that they are true; you forget that they are judgments and treat them as if they are facts. Forgetting that you create the ungrounded assessments often results in suffering.

Knowing the difference between grounded and ungrounded assessments may take some practice but, it is worth it. Grounded assessments will return you to earth as it is. Ungrounded assessments will lead you away from earth into a world of your own design, which you forget you created immediately after you have created it.

Grounded assessments will end arguments. Notice how many arguments are about ungrounded assessments. People are likely to argue over statements like: "He is nice," "You are late," "She is happy" or "They are rude." People are unlikely to argue over statements such as: "It is 60 degrees," "It is eight o'clock," "The corners of your mouth are turned up," or "He asked me a question," which are verifiable, sensory-based statements.

You may also want to notice that seemingly grounded observations like, "The sun is rising," are judgments which are not true but are based on our perspective. If you were standing on the north star, the sun wouldn't rise, and in fact, it doesn't rise here either.

The key to mastering your ability to live with the distinction between that which is grounded and ungrounded is to practice daily. By knowing which type of observation you are making, you will have a better idea as to whether you are in the real world (grounded) or in your own made up world (ungrounded).

If you look at life as a journey, knowing where you are is probably important. You would not call up a travel agent and tell her you want to go to New York without letting her know from where you will be leaving. When you are going anywhere, it helps to know where you are starting from. Practice in making the distinction between grounded assessments and ungrounded assessments will assist you in knowing where you are starting from and will even contribute to knowing where you want to go.

Grounded assessments determine our basic relationship with people and the world. Ungrounded assessments determine such things as what we buy, where we work, where we shop, and where we live. You are willing to pay more for a "good" car and less for a "bad" car. Thus, the ungrounded assessment "good" costs you money. If someone is "nice" to you, you will respond in a certain manner. Ungrounded assessments determine value and are important to the quality of your life.

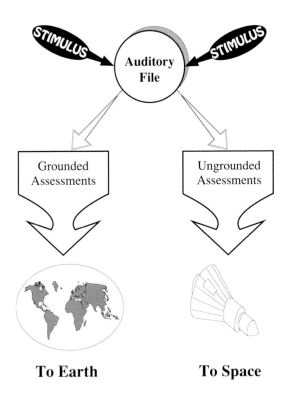

Illustration: Grounded - Ungrounded

Quality of life, by definition, is ungrounded. In grounded terms you might describe someone as alive, a lawyer, making $70,000 a year, and having a wife and two children. In ungrounded assessments you might say that he has a great life, a wonderful job, a supportive wife, two healthy, happy children, and a good income. Notice the difference between the two. Which person would you rather be? If you forget that the ungrounded one is just made up, you may forget what is real and spend your life pursuing the "right" ungrounded assessments. This pursuit often leads to problems in that there is no reality to the ungrounded assessments. They are phantoms not of this earth: figments of your imagination and other people's imaginations.

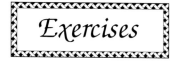

Look over your list of observations and discover which are grounded and which are ungrounded.

Find a partner and for one minute, look at your partner and make only **grounded statements** (sensory-based observations that twelve randomly-picked jurors would all agree were true). Then switch and have your partner make only **grounded statements** to you for one minute.

For one minute look at your partner and make only **ungrounded statements** (subjective interpretations, including the interpretations that you add to your grounded observations). Then switch.

Questions:

How much of your day was spent making grounded statements?
How much of your day was spent making ungrounded statements?
What did you notice during the exercise?
What was it like to make only grounded statements?
What was it like to receive only grounded statements?

What was it like to make only ungrounded statements?
What was it like to receive only ungrounded statements?
Which was easier?
Which was harder?

If your answers to these questions were ungrounded, then answer them again, taking care to make them grounded assessments.

The point here is not to come up with right answers. I don't know what the right answers to these questions would be. My guess is that the answers will be different for different people. That is typically the case. So, what did you notice? ... Of what you noticed, which of your observations are grounded and which are ungrounded?

3

Thinking

It is impossible to make sense of where you are without comparing it to other places you have been. The room is completely dark and silent. It is not possible to discern exactly what size it is, and it may not even be of a constant size. One thing you do know is here you are in this room. You think.

Your brain is the most amazing computer on earth. Your brain makes sense of the world throughout your life. Without it there would be no you, no thinking and no life, yet it functions without your understanding, respect or influence. It requires basic nutrition and that is all.

What have you done for your brain recently?

The world appears different to each individual, depending upon the range of ungrounded assessments he or she makes. What is a good car or a great job to one person may be a bad car or a hateful job to another. These differences are the result of a basic dissimilarity in what people perceive and how they make sense of it. The way you acquired your personal ability to interpret the world happened so quickly that you didn't even notice it while it was happening. There are billions of things that you could pay attention to at any given moment in time. The combination of your flashlight and your senses provide you with a system for filtering in specific information and filtering out everything else. This filtering system works similar to a pair of eye glasses which operate as a buffer between the world and the person wearing them, influencing every perception she has. You interpret the world through your eyes (visual sense), ears (auditory sense) and your nerves, skin, nose and taste buds (kinesthetic sense). You use the information from your five senses to allow yourself to make "sense" of the world and to be able to add meaning to your observations.

Around age six, people begin to prefer one sense over the others and spend the rest of their lives being more aware of either visual, auditory or kinesthetic data. Visual, auditory and kinesthetic data are stored in separate files in the brain. The following analogy is simplified, but it will illustrate my point. You have a sensory file filled with visual data. It contains pictures of everything you have ever seen in your life, both visual data you have seen through your eyes and imaginary images you've made in your head with your mind's eye. Every piece of visual data you have seen is stored in your visual file. This doesn't mean you can access every picture instantaneously when you choose, but the information is stored, nonetheless. In your auditory file you have stored every sound. These sounds consist of everything you have ever said and every sound you have ever made, out loud or internally, along with everything you have ever heard externally. You also have all of your habitual behaviors stored in your kinesthetic file. These are the movements that you have learned, such as, riding a bike, driving a car, walking, brushing your teeth and typing. Tastes, smells and physical sensations are processed in your kinesthetic file too, but these are not stored and are only experienced in the present.

Conservative scientists are saying that there are in excess of ten billion neurons in the brain while their less conservative colleagues are saying that there are three hundred billion neurons. We use the neurons to store, access and process all the visual, auditory and kinesthetic data in our brain. (It is possible that your brain does not actually store the data but tunes in to morphogenic fields that contain the data.)

The IRS only requires you to save your records for seven years; your brain saves all of your sensory stored data forever. Anytime anything goes on in the world around you, you sense and store it. An event happens; you attach similar pictures from the past to it from your visual file then run it through your kinesthetic file. The pictures you have attached inspire certain feelings. Then the event is run through your auditory file, and you attach stored words or sounds to it. Consequently you behave in a manner that relates to the way the event stimulated your files. There is no free choice involved whatsoever. This all happens in a fraction of a second—that is how fast the brain works.

Here is an illustration of how fast your brain runs:

PALCIP

Do you know what that word means?
Do you think that Palcip is a word?

How many words do you think that you have seen in your lifetime? Probably a lot of words, right? You read the word Palcip and then compared it to every single word that you've seen or heard in your whole life. How long did it take? Not even seconds. Less than a second. That is how fast your brain works.

Every time you sense something, you very rapidly run through your stored files and compare that thing with everything you have sensed before (and perhaps everything you anticipate you will sense). Depending upon how you sort your files, you will come up with certain opinions, judgments, grounded assessments and ungrounded assessments that determine how you perceive and interpret the world. The result of your file searches determines everything you say and everything you do in all aspects of your life. There are no moments in your life that take place without you searching through your files of stored data.

Everyone you meet or interact with has his own unique filing system, which differs in some respects from yours. Thus, other people live with very different perceptions of the world than you do. It may seem to you that your perceptions are the "right" ones to have, and you may even think that another person's perceptions are the same as yours. This is not likely since the information each of you has stored in your files is different.

I was in a restaurant and saw a young girl asking for a drink of her mother's soda. She let her mother know several times that she wanted some, but her mother was busy eating and didn't notice. Finally the little girl yelled. The mother reached over, hit the little girl on the side of the head and handed her the soda. This incident went into the little girl's files along with everything else in her life. Let's imagine that years later, she is on a date and her escort orders soda. All of a sudden, her brain returns to the auditory assessments she stored after being hit by her mother, and she finds herself upset and afraid of the person she is with.

Such an occurrence can happen easily since the brain is constantly sorting back over everything that has ever happened and attempting to make sense of the present by using past files. Anytime that anything in the present closely resembles something that has happened in the past, there is the likelihood that the brain will return you to whatever behavior allowed you to survive the previous situation. The behavior may not be appropriate, but to the brain, that is not important. The behavior worked before and you survived before. Thus, according to the logic system of the brain, the behavior must be repeated to ensure future survival, which is "all that matters." Rather than reacting appropriately in the present situation, you ignore what is happening and treat this as you did the earlier situation, reacting as you did before. This explains a lot of the strange behaviors people engage in. One of the functions of the brain is to come up with reasons and explanations for doing what you did in a specific situation. Given how quickly the mental process works, it is unlikely that you will come up with an accurate explanation, but you will always come up with some explanation.

Exercises

Watch someone do a certain behavior ... any behavior. ... Come up with a reason why he behaved that way. ... Make up a completely different reason for his behavior. ... Create ten more reasons which explain his behavior.

Think about something that you did today. ... Decide why you did that particular thing. ... Make up ten completely different reasons which explain your behavior.

Can you imagine yourself doing a certain behavior without having a reason to justify it? ... Can you think of behaviors that you do for no reason at all? ... What is more important: what someone does or the reason she did it? ... If someone is due to meet you at six o'clock and she arrives at eight o'clock with a good reason, will you be angry? ... It would probably depend on your assessment of how good the reason is. Meeting another friend and losing track of time is probably not a good enough reason for you, but a death in the family probably would be. Having a flat tire may be good enough unless she has a flat tire or car trouble often. Whether we like it or not, reasons make up much of the quality of our lives. Notice the gaps between your reasons and your behaviors. If you pay attention to your behaviors, you will automatically have reasons for them.

What would happen if you shifted your conscious focus and paid more attention to your behaviors rather than your reasons? ... What would happen if you declared yourself the director of your conscious focus? ... Could you focus consciousness on behaviors instead of reasons and explanations? ... What would that be like?

The next section will take you on a short adventure, journey onward.

3 1/2

Sense Adventure

$\mathcal{L}$et's take a short trip. Relax and get comfortable.

Imagine yourself walking to the nearest window. Outside the window is a beautiful, scenic view of nature. There are large trees and a grassy meadow all calling you to join them. There is a little dirt path leading into the woods and through the meadow. The sun is shining and the temperature is perfect. You find yourself magically transported onto the path. I'm not sure how you managed it, but there you are. You notice beautiful wild flowers growing along the path, and as you take a deep breath, you can smell their sweetness. You begin walking down the path to explore this wonderland.

You walk on, focusing your attention anywhere you choose, taking in a variety of smells, sights and sounds. After awhile you become aware of a sound in the distance, and your heart begins to beat a little faster in expectation. You have heard this sound before; there is a stream just ahead. It is flowing rapidly and you can hear it bubbling and gurgling. You think about walking a bit faster to get there sooner, but instead, you slow down a little to enjoy the sounds the stream makes as you get closer to it.

There it is. The stream is everything you expected and more. It is flowing very fast over countless rocks, ranging in size from boulders to pebbles. The stream is about fifteen feet wide, deep in some spots and shallow in others. The sun is reflecting brightly on the surface in some places, casting shadows in others. If you look closely, you can even see the shadows of little brook trout darting through the fast-moving water.

Isn't it amazing to see the amount of water that is going by all the time? ... Where does all that water come from and where is it going? ... This is exciting to think about. You wonder if the trout are having these same thoughts. They might just be having trout thoughts as they go about their trout days. Maybe they don't have to figure out the meaning of the stream or where it comes from. Maybe they already know, or perhaps they have other concerns. You might even imagine for a moment what it would be like to be a trout in the stream. How would life feel and look from their perspective, and how would the stream sound from the inside? ... Remember having had your own head under water and how it sounded? ... You might wonder how it sounds with trout ears.

•   •   •   •

And, so too flows your own *stream of consciousness*, going rapidly by while you sense small parts of it as it flows. You can only see a small part of what is really in your stream, and the more immersed you are in it, the more unique your perspective is. Your *stream of consciousness* probably has a beginning and an end just like the physical stream, only the beginning and end of your *stream* are not as easy to discover. You could hike to the source of the physical stream. It is not as easy to do so with your own consciousness because you *are* the *stream of consciousness* and the current (culture) is constantly pushing against you, allowing for little movement upstream. Most of your energy is spent attempting to keep your balance where you are. If you see any spot in your stream that looks a bit slower or safer, you move cautiously toward it, hoping to get a moment's rest from the flow. Each time you are ready for a rest, you discover there are no secure spots and you are always still in the flow. With practice, you may discover that you don't need to fight the current but, rather, that you can work with it.

I remember canoeing on a whitewater river early in the spring. I had very little experience canoeing on a fast, rock filled river. The person with me had even less. An experienced person would have had the sense not to even venture out on this river with an aluminum canoe. With the confidence of the truly ignorant, we started our adventure. About twenty yards downstream, we hit our first patch of rapids. I say "hit" because that is exactly what we did. The aluminum canoe hit the rocks, rode up on them and got stuck. Meanwhile, the current continued unabated. Hitting the back end of the canoe, the current pushed it sideways, allowing the flow of the river to rush into the boat. Seconds later we found ourselves chest deep in some of the coldest water I have ever felt.

At this point, the canoe was no longer interested in staying on the rocks; it started moving downstream. I decided this wouldn't do, so I braced myself against the rocky bottom to keep the boat, now full of water, from being swept away by the current. As I bounced along the rocks, unsuccessfully attempting to brace the boat, an intelligent idea occurred to me (perhaps the first intelligent one of the day). I stopped attempting to brace myself and floated with the canoe to a place where the current was slower and the water shallow. At that moment, I discovered that if you are stuck in a *stream of consciousness* (which you always are), it is best to ride it in the direction it is going. Attempting to fight the flow of the stream is counterproductive and may even be harmful.

Your *stream of consciousness* is flowing along at a rate in excess of 200,000 nerve firings per second, and any attempt to fight the flow will be exhausting, futile and possibly hazardous to your health.

For awhile, as I attempted to brace the canoe, the fear of being out of control was so great that I was willing to hurt myself in my attempt to be in control. This fear would have been there if I had been alone, but it was even more difficult to admit being out of control in front of someone else. As long as I needed to be in control, I had few alternatives but to fight the stream.

One of the predominant characteristics of our narrow beam of attention is that consciousness thinks that it is the boss and in control of everything. The purpose of consciousness is to run things (i.e. lose weight, quit smoking, get a job or have a relationship). Remember, however, that consciousness only has a narrow beam, so it will probably not control much, even though there is the appearance from inside the scope of the flashlight beam that consciousness controls everything.

In your stream, your narrow attention beam can only focus on one small spot at a time. This focus of consciousness is far from the source of the stream and you can't get to the source via consciousness. The narrow focus of your attention is designed to concentrate on whatever flows by. The flow is influenced by everything that goes on upstream: every rock, fish, breeze or change in the current. And yet when your beam of consciousness focuses on one area, the particular place you see appears to be all there is. The beam of consciousness can only focus on where you are; it cannot focus on or influence what happens upstream.

Behaviors are generated upstream and are observed when they flow into the focus of your beam of consciousness. The vast majority of your behaviors are generated and carried out without any conscious awareness whatsoever. My definition of the term rude is to bring into someone's conscious awareness a behavior that was previously outside it. Behaviors are generated and influenced well before they have the possibility of flowing into your focus. Although we have control over the judgments and opinions we make and reasons or explanations we give for our behaviors, we do not have control over our behaviors. Behaviors are generated upstream. The judgments, opinions, reasons and explanations make up our disposition over which we have conscious control.

Any attempts, through normal means, to influence what goes on upstream are futile and even counterproductive. They are similar to my bracing myself against the river bottom while attempting to hold the canoe in place. There are, however, ways you can influence what comes downstream to you, but you cannot act on them while you are attempting to brace the boat or while you are living with the illusion that you can influence your behaviors directly.

This book is about respectfully influencing the flow of your *stream of consciousness*, thereby indirectly influencing your behaviors. It is likely that over and over again you will find yourself braced against the bottom of the river attempting to prove that you are in control and that you can hold the canoe in place if you just exert enough energy. When this happens, let go and allow yourself to drift to a quiet shallow spot to get the water out of your boat, and dry off a little before attempting the next set of rapids. If you never braced yourself, you wouldn't get the wonderful opportunity to let go and trust yourself again.

•   •   •   •

Now remember that you are still standing at the edge of this beautiful stream, hearing the water rush by and seeing the sun playing upon the water.

After awhile you notice the shadows getting longer. You say good-bye to the stream. Take one more look, remembering that you can come back here any time you choose. You leisurely walk back down the path, looking at, listening to and feeling the wonders of nature as you go.

You find yourself standing in front of a window looking out at the woods. You find yourself a little bit older, a whole lot wiser, and ready to continue your journey upstream whenever you choose.

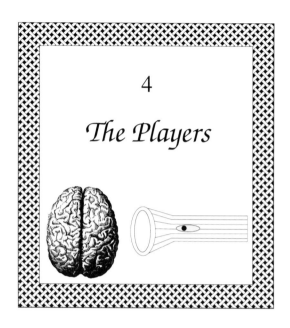

4

The Players

*But you are in luck. There are two different ways that you can determine what is in the room. You have a flashlight that will last for a long time and you have the ability to **trust** yourself. Your flashlight has a narrow beam and allows you to see only very small parts of the room at any point in time. The beam is so narrow that it is sometimes difficult to direct it right where you want it. You can only use this flashlight for a number of hours and then you must recharge it, which requires turning it off.*

The second way of knowing what is in the room is to simply trust that you know what is here. This type of knowing is not like the flashlight in that it seems much less tangible. All-encompassing trust is more uncomfortable than one little point of certainty, which the flashlight provides within a very limited context. Knowing by way of trust allows complete knowing of everything. To trust seems opposed to reason and logic, and the more you depend on your flashlight the more difficult this second way of knowing becomes.

We are taught consciously from the start to focus on what is in the narrow flashlight beam. Consciousness is slow to learn and slow to remember. The self is constantly learning everything available, with perfect recall. Perhaps we should attend to what the self is learning since it is the self that generates all of our behaviors.

Consciousness wants control of its surroundings. It wants to look good, prove how good it is, always be right and never make a mistake. It is constantly engaged with its own survival. The self does not care about looking good, surviving or being right. It continually maintains our lives and generates purposeful behaviors that consciousness then attempts to explain.

There are billions of bits of stimuli bombarding our five senses from the outside world at every moment in time. In order to cope with the constant flow of incoming information, we have developed the ability to let only a small part of this stimuli into our awareness. If people were aware of all data, everything in sight, all sounds, all sensations, every smell and every taste, they would be overwhelmed and wouldn't be able to cope with the world. It is a positive attribute to be able to filter this vast quantity of input and only pay attention to select bits.

The flashlight represents consciousness. The beam of light is analogous to the small amount of data consciousness can focus on. The flashlight is a tool, and like other tools, it is useful for certain functions and not for others. If used appropriately, your flashlight beam is very useful. If used inappropriately, it leads to all sorts of problems. The flashlight is very beneficial in that it has a limited beam which restricts the amount of information you have to juggle at one time. Without this limitation of conscious focus, you would be overwhelmed and unable to make distinctions.

The blessing of being able to focus on and to filter out excess data is also a liability in that whatever consciousness is shining on appears to be all there is. Consciousness constantly limits what you can be aware of by dictating your reality without your ever choosing how it sets limits. You must learn to live within these limits; to do so effectively you must discover how to move the flashlight in different directions and in different ways. You must learn to control how and where it is used as well as how you interpret what consciousness is focusing on. Interpreting that the flashlight is focusing on all there is leads to misconception and disappointment. If you continue to be aware that the flashlight is a limited light beam with more outside than inside its focus, the flashlight will be a useful and entertaining tool. Whatever is illuminated by the flashlight is what you are aware of and whatever is outside of it is what you are unaware of. What you are aware of, I call the gift of data received by consciousness.

Illustration: Conscious Focus

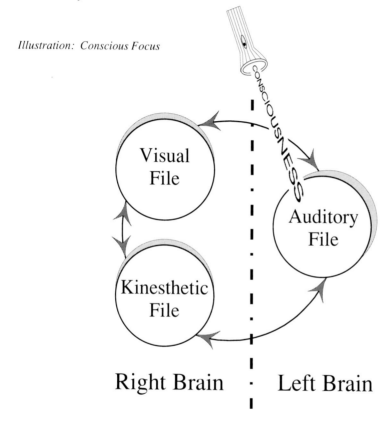

Consciousness focuses on a small part of your brain's activity. Consciousness can build constructs, but the only building blocks it has are sensory data. Its purpose is to form judgments, opinions and decisions out of the sensory building blocks. Consciousness is like a builder who is not aware of the blueprints or plans for the entire building but who is, nonetheless, continually working on random parts of the building. This random builder is always constructing something, but the constructs are not often a contribution to a finished project. Your ability to shift and effectively focus your conscious awareness determines the ease with which you move through life. What you focus on internally determines what you think and what you say. If you move your conscious focus, your thoughts change.

Focus of Consciousness

Possible Range of Consciousness

The Whole

Illustration: The Range of Conscious Focus

Consciousness can focus on the right or left side of the brain, but it has a bias toward the left side. Both sides of the brain store sensory data; you filter the data as you retrieve it but not as you store it. There is a division of labor between the two sides of the brain. As illustrated on the previous page, the left side contains auditory sensory data (sounds), which is everything you have ever heard both internally and externally. The right side of the brain stores all of your visual data (pictures) and kinesthetic data. While the kinesthetic stores rote daily routines and habitual behaviors, it also processes all of your physical sensations, smells and tastes.

One type of sound that the left side of the brain stores is language. Language is used to judge, evaluate, distinguish and fragment perceptions. The only way consciousness ever knows anything is in relation to something else. The role of consciousness is to make distinctions through language. Its job is to label and identify experiences so that behaviors can be explained and rationalized. Through the use of language, you keep track of all that has been or will be in your flashlight beam. The left side of the brain is reason-able: able to come up with reasons to fit any occasion. Its main occupation is understanding, reasoning and explaining.

When you were a young child, you learned that if you had a good enough reason for doing what you did, you could avoid negative consequences. If at age four or five you broke a vase, one of the first things your mother said was, "Why did you do that?" What she was really saying was, "Give me a good enough reason for what you did and I will go easier on you." You learn that if you have a good enough reason to explain a behavior, then the reason is more important than the behavior. You begin to focus your awareness on what you say rather than what you do. You focus your flashlight on the left side of the brain and ignore the right side. Your behaviors continue to create reality while your reasons build illusions.

The right side of your brain processes feelings (physical sensations) and stores visual data (pictures). The moment you sense something through your eyes, ears or body, the data goes directly to your brain and is stored in the appropriate place for that sense. In this process of filing, the new data is compared to all other data already stored and filed accordingly.

As the caretaker of physical sensations, the right side of the brain is responsible for all behaviors. Before you can behave, smell, taste or even move, your body checks with your kinesthetic file. Just as understanding is important to the left side of the brain, so is flexibility important to the right side. By generating different responses and exhibiting flexibility in behavior, you feed and nurture the right side of your brain. Very often, you don't become aware of behaviors until you find yourself engaging in them. Motions and series of movements are behaviors generated from the right side of your brain. Most of the movements you are good at (such as golf, tennis, ballet, walking, bicycling, driving and reading) were cumbersome initially. While you are becoming good at something, you may use the reason-able left side of your brain to focus on particular small parts of what you are doing. Chances are that while you are learning something new, you will be awkward at first and ill-at-ease. Grace and ease come after the new behavior shifts from a left brain—**cognitive function** to a right brain—**behavioral function**, unencumbered by language. Behaviors flow smoothly from the right brain and usually only draw left brain attention when something goes wrong. The idea that something is wrong is an ungrounded assessment made by the left brain.

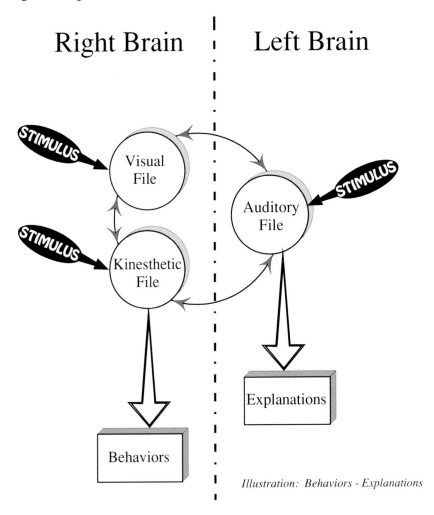

Illustration: Behaviors - Explanations

　　　The reason-able (left) side of the brain usually receives conscious attention while the behavior-able (right) side goes unnoticed until after a behavior is produced or an action takes place. Think of sitting in a chair and deciding to stand up. Which muscles tighten first? Focus your awareness on your physical sensations precisely as you begin to stand up. Notice how complex the activity of standing up is. It would take you years of study to figure out and understand all that happens in the action of standing up. Rather than focusing awareness on the physical sensations of standing up, we focus on the decision to stand up and trust that we will stand. The more you become aware of the complexity of sensations in the simplest movements, the more respect you will have for the right side of your brain.

We can see the difference in the way the two sides of the brain operate by looking at the way a person plays tennis. As you get better and better at tennis, it becomes more of a right brain function and you automatically hit the ball. You've made a particular shot so many times that you know how to behave when the opportunity arises to make it again. Your play improves as you become less and less aware of how you are hitting the shot. Let's say you are playing tennis with a friend. "That was a great forehand," you say to him. "How did you do that?" He begins to think with the reason-able side about exactly how he hit his forehand. His forehand, which had been on the behavior-able side, now moves into the reason-able side and becomes awkward as he analyzes and focuses his flashlight on it.

You can focus your flashlight beam (awareness) on five to nine bits of data at one time. Bit size varies for different people in different situations; it could be one digit or a whole phone number.

While learning tennis, it is useful to focus your awareness on certain parts of the game, but while playing a match, it is more useful to play and just let the behaviors flow. Virtually every sport requires doing the exact same movements in just the same way over and over. Consciousness gets in the way of being able to repeat them exactly. The ability of consciousness to judge and evaluate what you are doing interferes with the very behaviors you are evaluating.

Consciousness operates and focuses slowly compared to other brain processes. The brain has many functions on which it cannot or does not focus. Every moment you do wondrous things that are far beyond the capacity or view of consciousness. If I were to ask you, "Could you quite accurately measure two-thousandths of a second without any sort of automated device?" would you be able to? Using the right side of your brain (the behavior-able side) you can measure approximately two-thousandths of a second very easily. With the left side, it is impossible. To measure two-thousandths of a second, take your little fingers and touch them together. Can you tell which finger you feel sooner? If you are like most people, you feel both fingers at approximately the same time. Then take one of your little fingers and touch your lip. You will feel your lip two-thousandths of a second sooner than you will feel your finger, the difference being the time it takes the nerves to transmit the message to your brain, about two-thousandths of a second shorter from your lip to your brain than from your finger to your brain. Thus you have measured two-thousandths of a second. It didn't take a lot of thought or study or require the use of any measuring devices; instead, you took advantage of your built-in abilities and perceptions. You have a surplus of natural built-in abilities that go unnoticed and unappreciated by consciousness.

Another example of how to turn a task over to the behavior-able portion of the brain is to yawn. Attempt to yawn until you are successful. As you practice this, you will discover that you may initially pretend to yawn by holding your mouth open or by breathing in a particular way. But at a certain point, you really do yawn. You shift from pretending to actually yawning. Once it is a real yawn, it runs its course through to the end. The exact point at which the pretend yawn becomes a real one is where the shift from the reason-able to the behavior-able portion of the brain occurs. The behavior-able portion of the brain is automated. An automated process is one done without the focus of consciousness. Imagine if all parts of your life were as easy and effortless as yawning or breathing.

Both sides of the brain are important to living; the relationship between the two determines your quality of life. If consciousness operates as though its narrow beam is all there is and its judgments and evaluations are accurate, then life becomes difficult. If consciousness shows trust and respect for what is outside its focus, life gets easier and better. When you focus more on behaviors and less on judgments and explanations, life gets better yet. The relationship between what you are aware of and what you are not aware of requires the constant attention of consciousness. Given conscious attention, this relationship will grow and develop.

The brain operates so rapidly that to us, attending to the relationship between the reason-able and behavior-able is not very simple. Any explanation or understanding of how the brain works would, by definition, have to come from the reason-able side of the brain and be in a verbal form. Unfortunately, a verbal explanation of how it works is a slow process. If someone is teaching you how to speed read, one of the first things she will want you to learn is to read without saying the words to yourself. Saying the words slows down the reading process. Explaining how the brain works does not adequately reflect the behavioral functions of the brain. The brain works rapidly and the explanations of how it works come so slowly that the difference between the two is significant.

The capacity of the brain is determined by the interactions of neurons. You have hundreds of billions of possible interactions at any point in time.

This complexity defies explanation. You are already so good at thinking that any attempt to reasonably explain how good you are falls short of the behavioral evidence of your competence.

Notice the length of time it takes a light to turn on after you flip the switch. It's a very short length of time, too small for us to be reasonable about. Turn on the light switch and attempt to focus your awareness on the gap of time between the instant you turn the switch on and the moment the light illuminates the room. Your brain is much faster than the electric current that connects the switch and the light. Your ability to move and focus consciousness is much slower than the speed of the brain. Consciousness is an observer that is always behind brain function. Consciousness cannot directly influence the processes of the brain, but what it focuses on determines the grounded and ungrounded observations you make about everything in your life.

Think of a diver, using over 600 muscles in unison to perform a particular dive. How long would it take to explain what the diver is doing and how short a time does it take to execute the maneuver? There may or may not be very much in common between the behavior and the explanation. The explanation comes about after the behavior and is a conscious attempt to understand the behavior. The creation of explanations and reasons is a habit of consciousness. This habit is done for the sake of consciousness and does not directly influence behavior.

We go around behaving in ways that result in what we do and have in our lives. Buying things and picking a particular career or spouse are all the result of our behaviors. These activities are generated by the behavior-able portion of the brain. We also have judgments about and make decisions regarding our possessions, our careers, and our spouses. These are generated in the reason-able part of the brain. We often think that we know why we behave in a certain way and have explanations to support our actions when, in fact, it is the right side of the brain that comes up with the behavior and the reason-able portion that comes along afterwards to explain the behavior. And that's why you always get one of two things in life. **You either get what you want or you get the reasons for not having what you want.**

Getting what you want is made possible by the behavior-able portion of your brain. The reasons you don't have what you want are created by the reason-able portion of the brain. The further your explanations for your behavior are from the truth or the more thoroughly you believe your own reasons, the worse your life gets. Harmony between the reasons and behaviors leads to mental fitness and a life of ease.

Difficulties in your life can be traced to the relationship in your own brain between the reason-able left brain and the behavior-able right brain. As they relate better, you will have better relationships with other people, enough money and exactly what you want. The gap between what you say and what you do will shrink, and the quality of your life will get better.

One of the ways to expand and enjoy your life is to practice focusing your flashlight (consciousness) on seeing, hearing, feeling, smelling and tasting.

Exercises

Set aside an evening for exploration. Make sure that you stay up for at least a couple hours after dark. During that time, use a flashlight (a real one) for everything you do. If you read, do it with the flashlight. Do not watch television or work on a computer as both of these are light sources. Take a walk outside with your flashlight. Notice the limits of the flashlight beam. Notice that you have opinions about this exercise. You may think it is an adventure or you may think it is a waste of time. Yet it is the same exercise; only the judgments are different.

You may recall playing and exploring with a flashlight as a child or playing flashlight tag with friends. You may want to consider the flashlight as an alternative to having no light at all. Notice that if you compare it to having a lot of light, it seems inadequate, but if you compare it to being in complete darkness, it seems quite useful.

Remember that, in life, consciousness is like the flashlight. It constantly limits what you can be aware of. It limits you from focusing on "good" things and "bad" things. Its focus is constantly changing.

With your flashlight, pretend that your arm has a mind of its own: walk around in complete darkness, except for the flashlight, while moving the flashlight randomly as you walk. . . . Try putting your hand over the end of the flashlight partially obstructing the beam. . . . Turn your flashlight off for a while, and then notice your opinions about the flashlight when you turn it back on. . . . Make up your own flashlight games as you have made up your own games with your focus of consciousness.

Some people move their flashlights (focus of consciousness) randomly. Other people hold tightly to consciousness and move them as little as possible. Some people continually look where their flashlight beam is not while others don't know when their flashlight is on and when it is off. You may say, "He is in the dark about that." Some people move their flashlights so slowly they never catch up with enough different data to be interesting or interested. Other people move their conscious focus so rapidly they distract themselves and everyone around them. The way people focus and move their flashlights is habitual and influences their whole lives. With practice, you can learn to move your flashlight appropriately and efficiently.

5

Senses

There is no light and no way to tell where you are. It is impossible to make sense of where you are without comparing it to other places you have been. The room is completely dark and silent.

Your senses are your main filter for sorting through data about what is happening in the world and within you. They are your link with all that is. Your senses are what the brain uses when you think. We delude ourselves into thinking that thinking is more complicated than the senses.

*T*hink of the smell of freshly baked bread. Notice that as you do, you have pictures and sounds associated with the smell.

Think of a stove. ... Are you aware of the kind of stove you made a picture of as you read that sentence? ... Do you think other people made a picture of the same stove that you did?

Think of the sound of a fingernail scraping on a blackboard. ... What pictures and feelings do you associate with the sound?

What is a lake? ... Depending upon your experience with lakes, your pictures, words and feelings about lakes will be different from those of someone who has had experiences unlike your own. If you live on Lake Superior, a lake for you is probably huge, deep, cold and relatively clean. If you are from a city in the South, your lake is probably warm and small. If you are from Northern Canada, your lake may be frozen. In making sense of the world, you do not do it based on the world itself as much as on the sensory data you have stored about the world.

What does a northern lake sound like during the winter? . . . If you have never been on a lake when it is freezing, you probably have nothing in your auditory file to refer to. Anyone who has been around a lake as it freezes will have stored the incredible cracking, screaming, popping and explosive sounds a lake makes as the ice expands with the power and force necessary to move the entire frozen sheet. You cannot conceive of the sounds if you have never heard them, and you can not completely forget them once you have heard them.

At every moment in time there are billions of bits of information available to the five senses. People make "sense" of the world by receiving input through their five senses (sight, sound, smell, touch and taste). The amount of data they are aware of depends on how much room they have in their conscious focus. Consciousness focuses on a tiny amount of input from one, two or even three of your senses at any point in time. What your consciousness is focused on is your reality at that moment. What you do not focus on gets filed directly into your brain without being filtered and is stored without the focus of consciousness.

If a person has been sitting in a chair for a while, he might not notice the feeling of his feet resting on the floor. Although the sensory information is reaching the person's brain, after awhile he no longer pays attention to it consciously. If there is a constant sound in a room, such as a fan or blower, you will not be consciously aware of the sound after awhile. Consciousness is forever moving and shifting its focus. As goes consciousness, so goes your perception of reality. Your perception of reality is constantly changing and in a state of flux. But, as you attempt to keep today the same as yesterday, your "view of reality" may appear constant. To prove that you know what is happening and that you are in control of what is going on, you must keep your reality as constant and as much like the reality of others as you can. The variation of our perceptions of reality is a source of fear. Since other people's perceptions are different from yours, they are a constant threat to you. Consider for a moment how different people's perceptions can be in the same situation.

Imagine that you are on a beach at dusk. In each moment you may be filling your entire five to nine bits of conscious focus with information from your eyes: the beauty of the sunset, the colors of the clouds, the bright beautiful pinks, oranges, golds and purples in the sky. Meanwhile there may be waves lapping against the shore and sea gulls calling. You may not be aware of these sounds since at the moment your consciousness is being filled with data coming in through your eyes. You may see the waves or the gulls but not hear them.

You may have missed the feeling the breeze rolling off the water and brushing against your face, again because you were attending to your visual file. If, later on, you are telling someone about the sunset, you will probably tell her about what you saw. You would be less likely to report on the sounds or feelings of the beach, which someone else may have noticed. The information from your ears and nose and body has been stored in your brain, but since you were consciously paying attention to the visual data, you are less likely to recall the other data or report on it later.

Another person on the same beach may be conscious of the sounds. Her report about the evening on the beach would include information gathered by her ears: the waves lapping against the shore, sea gulls calling, the wind roaring, children laughing and squealing, sea lions barking, and a fog horn sounding.

If you meet this other person and discuss the sunset at the beach, your perceptions of what was there will be very different from hers. They may be so different that it may seem like the two of you were not even at the same place. What is different is the consciousness of the perceiver; it is unlikely that the beach scene itself was different. If there had been a third person present who had focused on kinesthetic stimuli, there would be yet another report about the beach. The kinesthetic report might be about the sensations of the sand on this person's bare feet and about the change in temperature that accompanied the sun setting and how the sun was warm on his skin before a coolness slowly poured upon him. There are at least as many different perceptions of a beach as there are grains of sand on the beach.

The likelihood that the consciousness of another person is filled with the same information as yours is about as likely as winning a lottery where there are billions of tickets being sold every single second, and only nine people can win.

We call it communication when we think that something in our consciousness is similar enough to someone else's that she supports our perception of reality. As we get older, we learn to be more satisfied with less similarity or, in extreme cases, we begin to imagine that other people really do think like we do. The acculturation process is an attempt to keep certain opinions and judgments so constant that we lose the ability to perceive them and no longer focus consciousness on them. Without the focus of consciousness, these opinions and judgments enter our brains unfiltered and become a part of our permanent reality. When you are communicating at the level of content, your conversation is taking place from consciousness. Communication from consciousness is an attempt to have another person's consciousness focus on the same spot as yours. Given the speed of the brain and your background of stored data, this is not likely. The best you can do is hear what you hear when someone else speaks since you will not hear what that person is saying.

From the time a child is born to the age of six or seven, he interprets the world with all five senses equally: sight, sound, touch, taste and smell. He has the ability to move his conscious focus rapidly with no preference to what sense it is on. By the age of seven, he has had enough contact with culture (the constant judgments and opinions) and the sense perceptions of the people around him (models) that he usually limits his everyday use of consciousness to one sense. If something very unusual or shocking happens, he may focus on one of his other files. People start to be more comfortable with having their flashlights on one sense and will continually keep them there. This repetitious focus becomes more and more habitual and limiting with repeated practice.

Some people limit themselves to what they see. They are less aware of the input available to them about what they feel or hear. Other people may be primarily aware of what they hear. Their consciousness is limited to sounds. These people will not be aware of many pictures or feelings. Still others may limit their consciousness to feelings.

Our brain works like a system of files. We have one file for everything we have ever seen, which contains all of the information we have taken in with our eyes (external) and the information we can visualize in our heads (internal). We have another file for sounds. This file holds all of the sounds you have heard or made up, both internally and externally. The third file contains feelings, smells and tastes.

Illustration: Stream of Consciousness

Stream of Consciousness

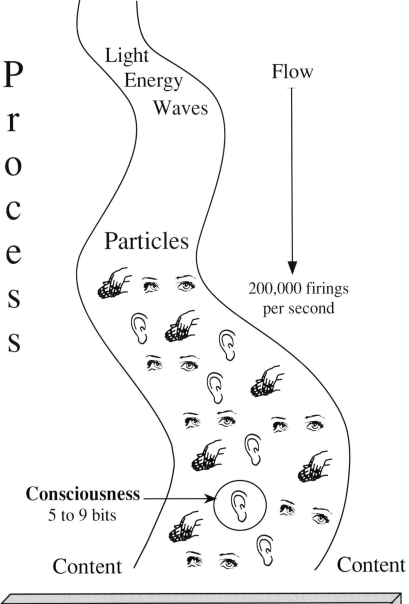

P
r
o
c
e
s
s

Light
Energy
Waves

Flow

Particles

200,000 firings
per second

Consciousness
5 to 9 bits

Content

Content

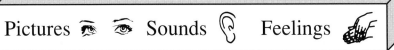

Pictures   Sounds   Feelings

We have access to our sensory files in relation to what we were conscious of when we filed the data. A person who is primarily aware of seeing the world will have a very well-defined path and easy retrieval access to her file of pictures. She will be very fluent with pictures and will think differently from someone who has a well-defined path to his file of sounds or feelings. A person will have better access to the file that corresponds to the sense she is most aware of.

All three of the sensory files continually influence our behavior. There is not a "best" file; that will depend on the situation you are in and the people around you.

If you focus primarily on sounds, you have, nonetheless, stored all the pictures and feelings of every situation you've experienced. Your **behaviors** are based on all of the data from all three files. Your **consciousness** bases its judgments, opinions and decisions on the small amount of data that comes from whichever sense it is focusing on at the time. Even the person who is very aware of sounds and is used to focusing consciousness on what she hears generates behaviors from all three sensory files. She quickly discovers that her explanations do not fit with her behaviors. She must focus consciously on her behaviors or on her explanations. If she focuses on behaviors, she will return to earth. If she focuses on explanations, she will build a world of her own illusion.

You would not send letters with just a name on them and expect them to arrive at their destination. It's more likely that the letter will get to a specific place if you add the address and even more likely if you also include the zip code. To attempt thinking (consciously) without being able to focus on all three files is like attempting to mail a letter with just a name. To communicate with someone using only your preferred focus is unlikely to reach him just as a letter addressed with only his name will probably not reach him. By practicing flexibility with your consciousness and developing the ability to focus on all three sensory files, you will be more accurate in all of your judgments and perceptions. You will be able to communicate effectively with almost everyone.

The basis of communication may be reaching a compromise between what you are aware of and what the person you are communicating with is aware of. Realizing the way your brain works gives you tremendous possibilities for expanding the variety of information you are able to focus awareness on. Expanding your awareness of the world around you allows you to become flexible enough to alter your consciousness and further your communication with yourself and other people. When you match someone's process or communicate through the same sensory filter that a person is using to interpret the world, that person will understand you better. You will also understand yourself better and avoid situations like the following.

I had a teacher participate in a workshop I was leading who was very aware of conversations in his head but unable to focus his flashlight beam on the pictures. As I watched him, it was easy for me to determine that one picture was running over and over in his brain and that he was not aware of the picture. As he practiced focusing on his visual file, he became aware of the picture that kept running: an image of an accident he had been in several years earlier. Every time this picture ran outside of his awareness, he would get upset. He would then try to find the reason he was upset. He was ready to quit teaching and was having trouble in his marriage, and he *knew* that was why he was upset. What was happening is that the picture would run, and since he had to find a reason for being upset, he would blame whatever was handy. Thus he blamed his job and marriage. After increasing his visual ability, he began to enjoy his teaching and his marriage. After he became aware of the picture, it stopped running over and over. We influence what we become aware of simply by becoming aware of it. We cannot accurately predict what the influence will be, however.

Increasing flexibility of sensory access contributes to the quality of your life. Dissatisfaction may be caused by your saying *bad* or *less than glorious* things internally without being aware that you are saying them. The sound track in your head influences your behavior whether you are aware of the track or not. Over the years, I have discovered that if people are having a difficult time, it often stems from what they are saying to themselves inside their own heads and outside of their conscious focus.

Once you have practiced focusing on specific senses, you will be less likely to be misunderstood by people. You will have more data and more relevant information allowing you to make informed decisions about what is happening. Your ability to think and act effectively depends on your ability to go to the sensory file where the appropriate data is stored. Imagine an office with a random filing system where it is impossible to search through all the file drawers available. If you cannot focus on all the sensory files, you might reach the conclusion that a certain file is not there. You would make decisions based only on the information you can find in the file that you are familiar with. Information in the other files might be very important and relevant to the work you are doing, but if you cannot have access to them, you will have to struggle along with the data you have.

Let's do a short exercise: take your hands and raise them high over your head. Look up at your hands. Keep your hands way up over your head and keep looking at them. Now, get depressed. Keep looking at your hands and, if you can, get very depressed.

It is not easy to get depressed in this position; looking up puts you in your picture file. Generally, when you look up you are making or storing pictures in your head. Pictures by themselves are just pictures. What makes a picture glad, sad or depressing is what we say about the picture or what we feel after seeing it. So a picture is not good or bad until you put a label on it. Prior to your assigning a judgment to the pictures, they are just pictures. Very seldom will you see someone looking up who is depressed or upset. A depressed person will look either down and to her right or down and to her left. The act of raising her eyes up will usually change her mood at least temporarily. If you are conversing with someone who is depressed, you can stand up so she must look up at you; as she looks up, she will be less depressed. You can also match her body position and then lead her to a different posture by altering your own.

Matching of senses is polite. If you were talking to someone who only speaks German, it would be polite to speak German to him. If you are speaking to someone who focuses mostly on the sound file, it would be polite to use the same language with him and to join him in filtering the world through your sound file, at least initially. Joining him in his preferred sensory file is like saying hello. After you have said hello, you can go into any of your other senses.

Basic rapport starts with saying hello to people in the sense they are focusing on consciously. Once you have established rapport with them, you can then run your own sequence of senses, as they run theirs. You only need to re-establish rapport when you notice that you are not being understood or that you cannot understand the other person.

Matching or mirroring which sensory filter a person is focusing on is one way to use awareness of the sensory files persuasively. Notice whether a person is seeing, hearing or feeling most often and do that back to him. You only need to match that person a little bit, just to be polite or to establish rapport, and then continue with any of the senses you want. You can also notice the combination of seeing, hearing and feeling that people do when they are in a good mood. People may purely see pictures when everything is going well. So you may want to spend time around them seeing pictures or images in your own head. Thus, that person may be more aware of pictures when he is around you and be in a good mood more often. Communicating with someone in his own language is much more effective than communicating in a different language.

If you aren't aware of which senses someone uses to make *sense* of the world, you are in constant danger of inadvertently offending or upsetting him. If you become aware of the senses and practice being able to focus on all of them, you will be more resourceful yourself and much more effective with others. In the next three chapters we will explore each sensory file in depth and practice focusing on each one.

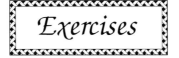

Read the following list of words. As you read each word, sort through every picture, sound and feeling you have ever had to understand the word. Do this instantaneously. Make sense of the word and then go on to the next word.

Moon	Cow	Deer
Soon	Late	Banana
June	Powerful	Frastas
Angry		Oven

How do you think about the words? . . . What senses or combinations of senses do you use to make *sense* of the words? . . . Do you make a picture of a deer? . . . What does your cow look like? . . . What color is it? . . . Where is it? . . . How do you think of June? . . . Do you see a calendar? . . . Do you see a typical June in your head? . . . Do you talk to yourself about some particular June in your past or future? . . . Is the moon full or some degree of less than full? . . . What is Frastas? . . . Do you have any pictures sounds or feelings associated with Frastas?

Think of words, situations, things or people that have special significance to you. What senses are you aware of using when you think of these?

How can you tell the difference between what is significant to you and what is not? ... How can you tell the difference between something that you like and something that you don't like? ... How do you know the difference between something that happened last week, something that happened last year and something that has not happened yet? ... All of these distinctions are made with your senses, not with your reasoning. Continue to explore how you make sense of your world.

Think of the best times you have ever had. ... Dwell on those times and discover how you were using your senses. ... Try applying the same sensory usage to new situations.

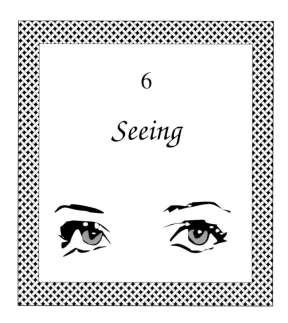

6

Seeing

The main communication tool in the brain is pictures. In order to make sense of the world, we create pictures. These visual representations are not the world; they are symbols which we use to represent it. We never see anything in the world itself, we see our internal visual representation of the world.

Can you tell the difference between a deer and a cow?

To answer the question, you must first hear it with your auditory sense and then make a picture of a deer and a picture of a cow in your brain. You must compare these two pictures and have a conversation with yourself about the similarity and differences between the pictures. The result of the comparison is a feeling about how different the two pictures are. You then have an auditory response: the answer to whether or not you can tell the difference. Your answer will depend on the pictures you make, the conversations you have, and your feelings. Isn't it amazing that such a simple question requires so much processing in the brain? You are not aware of all of this processing and you don't need to be. Different people will be aware of different parts of the processing, but people will search back over everything in their files to come up with a response.

If you have never seen a cow, you will not be able to answer the question because you will not be able to find a picture of a cow in your visual file. If you have only seen deer in cartoons, you will bring up a picture of a cartoon deer. If you are from the Western United States, you will probably have a picture of a mule deer while a person from the East will probably see a whitetail deer. Santa may see a reindeer. Your answer to the question of the difference between a deer and a cow will depend on what your pictures look like and how effective you are at focusing your consciousness on them.

Well, can you tell the difference between a deer and a cow?

How about from a distance of two miles ... or five years after it has died ... or a week after it is conceived? What at first appears to be a simple question can get more complicated depending on how you focus your consciousness to answer it. Notice that for each of the conditions stated above, you went on a separate and different search of your files. The searches were for distant, dead and zygotes of deer and cows. The content of the pictures, which will determine your answer, is dependent upon everything that has happened in your life, everything in your files and the way you sort through them. The question, expressed in language, is an invitation to go into your sensory files and discover what is there. When you go into the sensory files, you give clues about how you are using them. Just as a cow or a deer leaves tracks, you also leave tracks depending on the way you focus consciousness on the sensory files.

If you are practiced at focusing primarily on your visual file, you pay particular attention to what you see. You notice both internal and external stimuli represented as pictures in your head. At the level of process, if you prefer the visual file, you will give particular clues (listed below). People in the process of seeing pictures make certain gestures and behaviors which coincide with their use of visual sensory files. Here is a list of some of the gestures and behaviors.

Visual Clues:

• Eye Movements: Eyes above the horizontal or straight ahead with dilated pupils
• Head Position: Head tilted upward
• Breathing: High in the chest and rapid; shallow or repeated cessation of breathing for a moment or two

- Voice Tempo: Quick bursts of words; rapid tempo
- Tone of Voice: High pitched, sometimes nasal
- Skin Color: Paling of color
- Muscle Tension: Tight, high shoulders; tense abdomen
- Movement: Rapid and then pausing like a humming bird

Up and Right
Visual Constructed

Up and Left
Visual Remembered

Straight ahead and defocused
Visual Remembered

Illustration: Visual Eye Accessing

Some people will exhibit all of these clues as they focus on their stored visual data. Other people will display just one or two of these characteristics. With some practice, you will observe these visual clues easily. Sometimes they appear very briefly, but luckily, a person will repeat them over and over again as he thinks. If you miss something, wait twenty to thirty seconds, and the clues will present themselves again. If you are used to focusing on your own auditory or kinesthetic sensory files, the clues may be difficult to see. The exercises in this chapter will help you become more comfortable accessing your visually stored data.

The language a person uses is also a clue about which sensory file he is using. A person may not be aware that he is focusing on the sensory file, but he is still quite literal about which one he is using. When a person says, "Oh, I see what you mean," he may have just made a picture in his head to represent what you said.

The following is a list of words to notice and use when you are with someone who is aware of his visually-stored data:

see	reflect	spotless	stare
show	survey	glow	oversight
diagram	sketch	focus	illustrate
aim	ugly	obscure	neat
scan	shine	reflect	blind
perspective	vision	survey	appear
perceive	hide	sketch	stain
hazy	draw	observe	clear
envision	dull	reveal	cloudy
see at a glance	brilliant	view	image
picture	dimness	visible	pretty
gaze	opacity	watch	light
blush	cloudiness	foggy	sight
pattern	viewpoint	dark	portray
glimpse	illuminate	reveal	dim
look	glare	bright	

Listen for these words. They often indicate that someone is using his visual file. Refer to this list as you practice the visual exercises later in this chapter.

There are times when it will be very useful to focus particularly on the sense of sight, such as when you need an effective spelling strategy. A person who is a good speller stores words in the form of pictures. If asked to spell a word, she will move her eyes up and see a picture of the word. She can then read the correct spelling of the word from a picture stored internally. Auditory and kinesthetic sensory files are not effective for spelling. Visual sensory files are a fast and effective way to store words, and it is possible to see a whole word and use up only one bit of your consciousness.

Seeing pictures is an extremely fast process. "A picture is worth a thousand words" is a true statement as far as the brain is concerned. A picture is worth many thousands of feelings. Seeing is not better than hearing or feeling, but it is faster for conscious to focus on, consequently making pictures is the most economical way to store a lot of data. Forming pictures is the main method the brain uses to encode data from the world. One picture contains a lot of information, yet it may use only one bit of consciousness. One sound

contains much less data; nonetheless, it still uses one bit of consciousness. Feelings contain even less data and are processed much more slowly by consciousness than are pictures.

Another example of the use of visual sensory files is to imagine that you are a barber or a hair stylist. To cut hair effectively and attractively, you must be able to see what a person's hair looks like now, and from that image you must be able to construct a picture of what you want it to look like when you are done cutting. You must also have the kinesthetic ability to guide your hands and arms to produce a haircut that matches the picture you have in your head. If the picture you have is attractive to people and you have the ability to make the completed haircut look like your picture, we call you a good hair stylist or barber. Your picture of the finished haircut, without the skill to bring it about, will result in your giving a bad haircut. Likewise, if the picture you have of the finished haircut is not attractive to many people, you will not be considered a good stylist. If you are not aware of your stored pictures of the hairstyle, you have to wait until the cut is finished before you know how it will look.

Someone who wants his hair cut has a picture in his head of how he wants his hair to look, based on his particular set of stored files. It could be a picture of how it was cut last time, a stored picture of how he wants it cut this time or a picture of some person he saw yesterday or last year. He will know whether or not he likes the haircut by comparing how closely it matches his picture. If he can focus on the picture of how he wants his hair and then communicate specifically how he wants it to look, he is more likely to get a haircut he likes. If he cannot focus on the pictures, he will not find out until after his hair is cut whether or not he likes the haircut.

A similar process goes on when you are arriving home to your spouse, having a birthday, buying a car, learning something or entering a meeting. You make pictures in each of these situations and then compare your pictures to what actually happens. You then talk to yourself about the comparison and have physical sensations about the similarities and differences between the pictures. The hair dresser needs a picture of what she wants the finished cut to look like, but she must also be able to determine what the client wants. She can give the best haircut imaginable, yet if the client's picture is very different from hers, the client may not like the haircut.

You may enter a meeting with pictures of how you want the meeting to go, but the other people in the meeting may have pictures very different from yours. You must learn to discern other people's pictures as well as your own.

If you cannot do this, it is unlikely that you will get along with or enjoy being with other people. By learning to observe what senses others are using, you will be able to join them in their world and communicate much more effectively. By practicing moving your flashlight on all three of your sensory files, you will be more flexible with your expectations.

When you first meet someone, you will have very few stored images of her. The longer you are around her, the more images you will have stored. How you access these stored files will determine which pictures you use when around the person. The longer you are with a person, the more difficult it is to see who she is now and the easier it is to interact with her strictly from your own files. The more you can observe externally how she is now or the more you access positive, happy pictures from your files, the better you will like the person. If you continue to see how the person is at the moment, you can be married to her for eighty years and still be interested and fascinated by her. The key to successful relationships is in the way the brain processes data.

The processing speed in your brain is so fast that before you can think or act, your brain has already made pictures of what you want to do or how you want things to turn out. You have pictures of what type of career you want, what you want your spouse to look like, what clothes you like, who you want to be friends with and where you want to live. These pictures result in expectations. To have an expectation means that you have determined how something should turn out. These processes of the brain are extremely rapid and take place beneath the level of consciousness. When you have determined how things should turn out, there is the definite possibility that they will not fit your pictures. You then have two choices: you can either change your picture of how things should be or you can decide that the way things turned out is really what you wanted. The latter choice will lead you into a world of illusion. The former opens the door to two new possibilities. You can continue to compare the picture of what you expect to how things are right now and judge that the wrong thing happened. Or, after the comparison is made, you can simply notice what happened and then move forward to the next situation for which you will have already developed an expectation. When you form expectations, there is a substantial likelihood that the world will not meet your expectations and you will be disappointed. There is also the possibility for things to turn out much better than your pictures and for you to be delighted. In any case, your attitude toward life is determined by the type of pictures you construct of your future or, in other words, by your expectations. If your stored or created pictures are not very positive, you will not expect much goodness

or greatness to happen to you and will probably be called a pessimist. If your pictures are of wonderful delightful happenings, you will probably be called an optimist.

The pictures you make are not of your choosing. They happen at brain speed. From your perspective some pictures will be better than others . The most effective way to deal with pictures is to practice with the visual file enough to become aware of the pictures as pictures. Be aware that things in the world are the way they are, that your pictures are the way they are, and that the difference between the two doesn't mean anything. The difference between the two is a constant invitation for you to miss how things really are and spend life attempting to have the world conform to your expectations. This can be a problem since your expectations change constantly and are at the whim of your sensory files. It is also problematic because the world does not care what your expectations are. Distinguishing between expectations and reality is as easy as becoming aware of your pictures.

Remember that whether you are aware of pictures or not, the pictures continue to influence your behaviors. Through practice in consciously using the visual files, you will be more aware of and alert to how things are. You will be able to discern between your pictures of the world now and pictures you have constructed of how the world should be. You will be able to choose your disposition toward the world now and what it will be in the future. Your disposition is made up of your opinions, judgments and decisions. It is initiated by the pictures you see and then determined by what you say about them. The pictures are not good or bad, right or wrong, or in any way qualitative, until you use the auditory file to put labels on them. The process of putting labels on pictures happens so rapidly in the brain that it is easy to think that the labels really represent the pictures themselves. Practice in focusing your consciousness will enable you to determine the difference between the pictures and the labels and allow you to interrupt the sequence of labeling the pictures and add new or different labels to them. By changing labels, you also alter your disposition, which increases your ability to choose between optimism or pessimism, happiness or sadness and joy or depression at any moment in time.

Exercises

Some people have difficulty becoming aware of the pictures in their heads. Other people are so aware of the pictures that for them, thinking is entirely composed of visual images. Remember that pictures are represented and used in your brain whether you can focus on them or not. If you have difficulty seeing your internal pictures, it will be useful to start out with simple images. Close your eyes. What do you see? . . . Is it dark or light? . . . Can you add a color to it? . . . Begin just with colors and work up to shapes. You may think the pictures should look a particular way or that they should be as vivid as what you see when your eyes are open. Although this may not be the case, with practice you will be able to focus on your pictures with ease. Imagine the fun of being able to lean back, close your eyes and see a movie in your head. In this movie you are the director and can have the actors be anyone you choose doing anything you want. This can be entertaining, educational, creative and inexpensive.

For one minute move your eyes up and to your left, which is the eye movement associated with visually remembered pictures. Breath high in your chest and lift your hands up as though they are pointing at pictures. Think of things you have seen (it might help to close your eyes). See things from your past, paying attention to colors, shapes, clarity, and other visual distinctions.

For one minute move your eyes up and to your right in order to access visually constructed pictures. Make up new pictures and see things you have never seen before. Continue to breathe high in your chest and have your hands up. Notice the differences between moving your eyes up and to the right and up and to the left.

For one minute look straight ahead with your eyes defocused. Look without really seeing what is in front of you. Continue to breath high in your chest. See pictures in your head. This is where you put your eyes to make all types of pictures, most of which are moving in quick succession and seldom enter awareness.

Look around you. What do you see? . . . Close your eyes and make pictures in your head. . . . Make a picture of a hippopotamus with roller skates . . . your best friend and your best friend riding the hippopotamus. Make a picture of someone that you have never seen before . . . someone that you think you will never see again . . . yourself as a baby . . . and yourself as a young child. . . . Finally picture yourself exactly the way you want to be.

Watch television with the sound off. Put ear plugs in your ears for fifteen minute intervals and notice whether your ability to see increases. Practice keeping your eyes looking upward for two minutes in succession. Practice the attributes of visual behavior for two minutes each morning. Look up throughout your day. Notice ceilings, clouds, tops of buildings, and people that are taller than you.

Watch other people to determine whether they are accessing their visual files by looking for visual movements and listening for the use of visual words.

Find someone who has his eyes up a lot and uses many visual words. Spend time with that person. Learn how to do what he is doing. This is best done just by being around him and matching some of his behaviors.

Listed below are a few do's and do not's for communicating with people who use seeing as their primary sense:

Don't

Don't stand closer than three feet directly in front of them.
Don't sit lower than they are sitting.
Don't deliberately tilt wall hangings around these people or arrive at their houses with a button undone.
Don't use your hands wildly in front of their faces during conversations with them.

(These actions will distract someone who is paying attention to the visual images he makes in his head. Standing right in front of someone who is practiced in thinking in pictures is like standing right on top of a professor's blackboard during a lecture. The waving gestures are similar to erasing the information from the blackboard.)

Do

Do keep things neat and looking good around them.

Do chew with your mouth closed.

Do stand next to them.

Do sit eye level or higher.

(Since a person who uses his sense of sight primarily needs to look up to get access to his visual data, sitting lower than that person makes it more difficult for him to see pictures.)

7

Hearing

When you are listening to someone, it is important to determine whether or not he knows what he is talking about. Opinions are everywhere, but relevant and informed opinions are rare. If you don't know the difference between the two, you will continually misjudge people and be misled. If you don't know the difference between constructs of your auditory track and reality, you will be your own worst enemy. If you do learn the difference, you will be your own best friend.

I have met people who are unaware that they speak to themselves in their own heads. I have met people who have constant hums in their heads and who cannot distinguish internal sounds and conversation from the hum. There are people who can listen to twelve different voices at the same time and distinguish the content of each voice and people who believe that everything they say in their own heads is true. Some people have the voices of their mothers or fathers in their heads, commenting critically on everything they do.

It seems that there is a difference between you and a duck or you and a dog. Imagine that you have an important meeting. You want it to turn out a particular way, but the meeting does not turn out the way you intended. You will probably be left with some conversations in your head: conversations about how you could have or should have handled the meeting differently, conversations about how you never get what you want and you lost again, or conversations about it not mattering anyway because soon you will be on to other things and who cares anyway. Each of these conversations reflects the point in your life at which you stopped maturing, and the constant reminder of your immaturity is brought to you courtesy of your auditory track.

Your auditory track is like a television commercial gone wild, you may not enjoy it, but you will put up with the auditory track and continue to listen as the voice comments on everything that happens. I don't think that a dog or a duck has this auditory track. Dogs and ducks just do what they do: they eat, move around and live their lives without the internal conversation. They eat what is there to eat without comparing it to what they ate last Tuesday. They sleep without worrying about resting comfortably or some big event the next day. The only time dogs and ducks worry is when you are around to attribute worry to them. A wild wolf eats what it can find. A domestic dog must have the latest food with the tangy taste of real beef and cheese bits. The difference is the imposition of our internal commercials on the dog. Because we are silly and think that our auditory commercials are relevant, the dog must find them relevant, too.

Internal auditory commercials are just one part of the auditory file. The file also contains every sound that you have ever heard. It contains things your parents said to you as a child and all the music you have ever heard. It contains all of the internal noises that are part of your body working. Bits of data from the auditory file are linear and contain much less information than your pictures. Auditory information must be accessed in particular sequences depending on how it was stored.

When a person is used to concentrating primarily on her auditory file, she pays particular attention to what she hears. She listens to both the sounds in her head and external auditory data. At the level of process, people who prefer to use their auditory files give particular clues. Attune yourself to these auditory clues to perceive people and yourself in the process of using the auditory file.

Auditory Clues:

• Eye Movements: Eyes down and to your left, level and to your left, or level
       and to your right
• Head Position: Level; tilted to the left; turned so that one ear is directed to
       the speaker

- Breathing: Even breathing from the middle of the chest
- Voice Tempo: Rhythmic, even tempo
- Tone of Voice: Monotone
- Skin Color: Even coloring
- Muscle Tension: Rhythmic, even movements and tension
- Movement: Foot, hand or leg tapping methodically

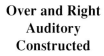

**Over and Right
Auditory
Constructed**

**Over and Left
Auditory
Remembered**

**Down and Left
Auditory Digital**

Illustration: Auditory Eye Accessing

When a person says, "That idea really sounds good," or, "That strikes a chord," she may have just processed your idea through her auditory file. The following is a list of words to listen for and use when you are with someone who orchestrates life auditorily:

babble	aloud	shrill	rasp	hear	resound
speak	lie	shout	sound	told	resounding
talk	chatter	tell	hiss	say	harmony
voice	silent	clang	noise	utter	vibration
boom	listen	tone	shriek	discuss	lend an ear
yell	moan	praise	clatter	chant	dissonance
listen	squawk	sing	scream	cadence	sounds like
snore	noisy	chime	silence	whine	acoustics
squeal	groan	purr	ring	grumble	verbalize
cry	debate	argue	whisper	describe	strikes a chord
music	loud	quiet	amplify	compute	orchestration
tune	call				

A person with a very well-developed hearing file will tend to talk more slowly than someone who is seeing pictures. When a person is using his auditory file, he will talk from the middle of his chest and usually have his hands somewhere around his ear, mouth or head. The pose of the thinker is one of someone who is paying attention to auditory information. He will listen specifically to what he is saying or hearing (both externally and inside his own head). He will usually speak in a monotone, using words from the above list and phrases like "that *sounds* good," "I'm sorry to *hear* that," and "you don't *say*." You may find this person tapping his foot or hand as he keeps an internal beat, thus sending information to his auditory file.

When you talk to yourself internally, the muscles in your throat make movements similar to those you make to speak externally. You may even notice that people don't breath when they are talking to themselves internally. Most people cannot breath and talk at the same time. Thus talking to yourself, in your head, restricts the amount of oxygen available to your body. If your thinking is limited to the auditory file, your oxygen intake is limited as well.

If you are unable to focus your consciousness on your auditory files, you will not be aware of many sounds or conversations in your head. Remember that what you are unaware of often has a greater impact on you than you are aware of. With practice you can learn to focus on different parts of your auditory file.

Most people carry less than glorious conversations learned early in life with them everywhere and listen to these internal auditory tapes any-where—anytime. Whenever the going gets tough, these negative conversations get louder and more prominent. If people are not aware of them, the conversations will influence their behaviors and alter their opinions and judgments. If people become aware of the internal conversations, they can have them go on without influencing their behaviors, opinions and judgments.

It is the nature of the internal dialogue to be critical most of the time. To counteract this phenomenon, we must first learn to hear the dialogue and then learn to put it in perspective. Internal dialogues are sequences of opinions and judgments that may have nothing to do with the present situation.

•   •   •   •

I'd like you to meet a friend of mine. His name is Jim, and he has thousands of dollars worth of stereo equipment, records and compact disks at home. He bought his house because it was on a quiet street in a quiet section of town. Jim enjoys the art of conversation and spends hours learning irrelevant facts so that he will know a lot about any subject that may arise in conversation. Arrangement of furniture and cleanliness are not important to Jim as long as his speakers are just the right distance apart. Jim is someone who prefers to interact with the world primarily auditorily and will listen very carefully to every word he tells himself. Depending on his disposition, he may or may not listen to external sounds. Jim can converse for hours without ever varying the pitch of his deep bass monotone. Occasionally he varies the speed of his monotone delivery thinking he is changing the pitch He keeps his hands somewhere around his head or ears. He is often in the pose of the thinker, with his head resting on his chin, deep in thought. Jim seldom hears what anyone says to him; rather he will usually hear what he says about what someone says. In other words, he translates other people's words into his own in order to hear them. This is a way of protecting himself from confrontation and a way to keep his opinions and judgments safe. Jim will not move physically or figuratively unless he can understand and figure out why he should. Thus he does not move around much or take part in many activities. Understanding concepts, ideas, and life for Jim is related to specific conversations in his head. He smokes cigarettes and has himself convinced that his lungs are beautiful and clean. "They must be because I say they are," says Jim.

Jim lives in a world based on his own auditory tracks with few distractions from the outside world. His idea of conversation is a monologue. His idea of life is words.

•   •   •   •

Most people you meet will not focus as exclusively on auditory files as Jim does. He is an extreme case of a person practiced in using his auditory data to the exclusion of his visual and kinesthetic data. Yet you will find many of Jim's traits in the people you know. The use of the auditory sensory file is the dominant tendency in the United States, followed by visual and kinesthetic files, respectively.

Many animals have a better-developed auditory ability than humans although I am not aware of any animal that has a language development comparable to that of human beings. Animals attend to sounds outside, while people are able to listen to the conversations inside their heads as well as external sounds. People pay more attention to what they say than what they do. If Jim can convince himself that it is safe to step off a cliff, he will step off. Most animals would not be so foolish.

Language determines the amount of suffering we will have in our lives. Have you ever cut your finger and not been aware that you cut it until you saw blood? Notice that until you discovered the cut, it did not hurt. Once you noticed it, the pain began. And the more you attempted to get rid of the pain, the more aware you became of it. The cut was outside your conscious focus and you only became aware of it when your flashlight beam focused on it. When your flashlight beam is on the injury, you have a cut and pain. When your flashlight beam is completely focused anywhere else, you just have a cut. The auditory track allows you to have the pain.

Throughout history, people have walked over red hot coals without burning their feet. This feat is done primarily by filling the focus of consciousness with particular visual and auditory data that have nothing to do with coals or burning. Blocking the kinesthetic file focus by filling your five to nine bits of awareness with visual and auditory data is mandatory for avoiding burning while walking on red hot coals.

You get a different sort of pain when a meeting does not go the way you wanted and often continue to have critical opinions and judgments about it. The opinions and judgments develop an existence of their own and may even seem to mean something about you. If persistent enough, these conversations will negatively influence the next meeting. It may be useful to attend to either your visual file or your kinesthetic file when your auditory is filled with negative opinions and judgements. Your auditory file is necessary; it is not an accident that you have it. Use the exercises at the end of this chapter to have your internal auditory file become your ally.

There is another group of auditory words that I did not mention earlier, those which comprise the language of emotions. Emotions are auditory labels that we use to describe events which originated in the kinesthetic file. These words may have initially coincided with feelings, but they very rapidly developed an existence of their own. Emotions are often inaccurately called feelings and identified with the kinesthetic file; however, they are not physical sensations. A person who confuses emotions and feelings will misread his files. This confusion has us think we are focusing on the kinesthetic file when we are actually focusing on the auditory file.

Here is a partial list of auditory file emotion words:

happy	love	bitter	mad
sad	stress	confused	guilty
glad	tension	delighted	joy
angry	depressed	rejection	helpless

The confusion regarding emotions and feelings is prevalent in our society, but the distinction between them is easily clarified and important.

Feelings: Physical sensations.

Emotions: The ungrounded assessment (label) we attach to physical sensations with the auditory file.

When we say we are happy or sad, we use these labels to justify our actions. We are powerless to influence emotions when we call them feelings. When we go to the feeling file, by saying for example, "I feel sad," we find nothing to focus on since *sad* is a label from the auditory file about physical sensations like warmth around your eyes and tightness in your belly. We thus claim that it is not our fault that we are sad or happy but that it is a condition brought about by something outside ourselves over which we have no control. The world and circumstances never influence our emotions since emotions are constructed in the auditory file. They are created by us through an auditory event called a declaration. Different people will assign different labels to the same circumstances. In the same situation, one person may be angry while another is confused. If it were the circumstance causing the emotion, there would be a closer correlation between the labels different people attach to the same circumstances. Emotions are personal judgments and opinions that we consider to be true: they determine our orientation toward life—disposition. If we experience them often enough, they become beliefs and determine our future perceptions. By focusing your flashlight beam of consciousness on emotions, you can identify them as the subjective labels they are. You will find emotions in the auditory file.

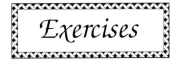

Exercises

For one minute move your eyes over to the right, looking in the direction of your ear. This is where you move your eyes when you are constructing auditory data. Breath evenly with your whole chest. Listen for either internal or external sounds.

For one minute move your eyes over and to your left, looking in the direction of your ear. This is the eye position for remembering auditory files. Breath evenly with your whole chest. Again, listen for either internal or external sounds.

For one minute move your eyes down and to your left. This is the position we are in when we listen to the critical internal auditory track we often identify as ourselves. Get into the "Thinker pose"; rest your chin in your hand, breath evenly with your whole chest and tap your foot. Listen for conversation internally.

Close your eyes and listen. ... What do you hear? ... Can you hear sounds and noises happening around you? ... Can you hear sounds from the past or from the future? ... Make the sound of roller skates on a sidewalk, hear your best friend talking, and hear your best friend talking while roller skating. ... Hear a voice you have never heard before ... a voice you never expected to hear again. ... Hear some words you have always wanted to hear. Listen to the sounds you made as a baby. ... Listen to the sounds you made when you were just learning to speak. ... Listen to the way you speak now. Listen to yourself speaking in your head.

As you listen to conversations in your head, become dubious of what is being said. Notice the tone of voice, tempo, volume, and other qualities in your internal voices in various situations. What does your voice sound like when you are happy? ... critical? ... sad? ... tired? Learn to vary the qualities of your internal voices and you will vary your emotional state.

Speak out loud and notice the qualities of your voice. Record your voice. Listen to the recording and hear the sound of your voice as other people hear it.

Listen to different types of music. Listen to music from other cultures. Take your local ethnomusicologist out to dinner and observe her behavior.

Have the television on with your back to it while you listen without watching. ... Listen to the radio. ... Close your eyes and practice life without external visual input. ... Meet someone new without the use of your eyes. Notice if you make a picture of the person in your head. ... Think of a time you spoke with someone on the phone and thought you knew what she looked like only to discover she looked nothing like you expected. Practice keeping your eyes horizontal and to the right for one minute, and horizontal and to the left for one minute (looking in the direction of your ears). Practice the gestures and clues of the auditory file for two minutes each morning. Listen throughout your day. Become aware of people's voices, the wind, the sound of appliances, all the sounds in your head and body, and the qualities and quantities of sounds around you.

Practice distinguishing between emotions and feelings. Say, "I am having a conversation about being angry," rather than, "I feel angry." Anger is not a physical sensation. Anger is an emotion, which means that it is an auditory creation and not a feeling.

Watch and listen to other people to determine whether they are making auditory movements. Find someone who has his eyes down and to his left, or horizontal to the right or left the majority of the time and who uses many auditory words. Spend time with that person. Learn how to do what he is doing. This is best accomplished just by being around him and matching some of his behaviors.

Listed below are a few auditory do's and do not's:

Don't

Don't make repetitious sounds around them, such as snapping your
gum, tapping your pen, or clearing your throat.
Don't make very loud noises in their presence.
Don't take long pauses in mid-sentence.
Don't whine or talk in a grating tone of voice.
Don't talk so softly that you can't be heard.

Do

Do complete every sentence you begin.
Do listen to everything this person says.
Do speak clearly and decisively.
Do or **Don't** give this person the silent treatment, depending on what
your purpose is.

7 1/2

Recitation

*P*lease say the following phrases out loud. Say each line until you can make that line true as it applies to you. Remember that I am not saying that it is really true; I want you to make it true by saying it. To make it true for yourself, it is necessary to have pictures, physical sensations and internal dialogues that correlate with what you are saying. Practice saying these lines with different pictures and internal dialogues until you think they are true.

These phrases are affirmations. If these are true for you and you say them, they will contribute to the quality of your life. If you say affirmations that are not true for you, your quality of life declines. If you affirm what is true, you return to earth; if you affirm what is not true, you leave the earth. The farther you are from earth, the more difficult it is to live.

I am only human.
I always do the best I can.
Sometimes I like what I do.
Sometimes I don't like what I do.
I wish I could always like what I do.
I wish I could always do what I like.

I have two ears.
I have two eyes.

I have one body.
I see much with my eyes.
I hear much with my ears.
I feel much with my body.
I notice some of what I see.
I notice some of what I hear.
I notice some of what I feel.
I hear none of what I see.
I usually think that what I notice is all there is.

I have judgments and opinions about everything.
I want my judgments and opinions to be right.
I would like to always know the truth.
I would like to be accurate all the time.
Sometimes I am right.
Sometimes I am wrong.
I don't like this, but I am only human.
I am only human.
I always do the best I can.
My best is just my best.
I have opinions about my best.
Sometimes my best is good enough.
Sometimes my best is not good enough.
I would like my best to always be good enough.
I want to always like myself.
I want to always trust myself.
I don't always like myself.
I don't always trust myself.
That is the way it is to be human.
I don't like it.
That is the way it is.
Life is precarious.
That is the way it is.

I am not sure how long I will live.
I might die in the next minute.
I might die in the next hour.
I might die in the next year.
I might live forever.

I might be proud of my life.
I might not be proud of my life.
I might not even be living now.
I want to know all there is about life.
I want to live my life to the fullest.
I am afraid I might not be living to the fullest.
I am afraid I might be living life to the fullest.
Sometimes I think I am in control of my life.
Sometimes I think I am not in control of my life.
Sometimes I reminisce about the past.
Sometimes I worry about the future.
I do not know what will happen in the future.
I wish I could trust that the right things will happen to me in the future.
I sometimes live in the present.
Living in the present is living before judgment.

There are other people in my world.
I did not choose to have all of these people in my world.
Some people I like.
Some people I don't like.
Some people I like sometimes and not other times.
I can never tell when I will like someone until I like them.
I wish other people were predictable.
I wish other people were more like me.
I wish other people would always do what I want them to do.
I wish I could have any type of relationship with anyone I want any time I want.
I wish I knew all about relationships.
I wish I could live happily ever after.
I wish everyone could live happily ever after.
I want other people to like me.
I want other people to love me.
Sometimes other people like me; sometimes they don't.
Sometimes other people love me; sometimes they don't.

I live on earth.
There are trees on my earth.
There are buildings on my earth.
There are people on my earth.
Some parts of earth I like and some I don't.

8

Feeling

You feel hot, cold, light or heavy. These are feelings. Feelings are physical sensations. Sensations don't mean anything or justify anything. You feel them in the present, and when they are gone, you forget them.

You use feelings to walk. You use feelings to talk. You use the auditory file for the content of speech but the kinesthetic file for the behavior of speaking.

The kinesthetic file is the source of all behaviors. From lifting your hand to walking to dancing, everything we do is based on and generated from the kinesthetic file. Kinesthetic data is responsible for most of what we call life.

You are a master of coordination. To lift this book an inch requires the coordination of about one hundred and fifty muscles. It takes thousands of nerve firings in your brain to coordinate these muscles. How do you coordinate all of these muscles at once and know in exactly what order to trigger the nerve impulses? How can you do all this without focusing your attention on it? Think of how easily you raise the book and the precision with which you do it; you have probably taken for granted how extraordinary and coordinated you are. Perhaps you can find a little time today to celebrate your dexterity and ability to move, which are gifts from your kinesthetic sensory file.

You learned to walk, using your kinesthetic data, before you developed the ability to judge and evaluate with your auditory file. You attempted walking many times before you were successful. Most of a baby's world and much of a child's world is based on physical sensations, smell, and taste.

I remember watching my daughter as a baby, attempting to pull herself up on a kitchen cabinet. It appeared to take all of her abilities and strength to pull herself to her feet. But the moment she got up, she placed one foot on the cabinet to climb higher. Without the interference of auditory judgments, the kinesthetic file learns rapidly and perfectly. Our bodies are a perfect fit for the world. We discover the world through the interplay of external stimuli with our kinesthetic file which contain nothing intellectual—only behaviors. The kinesthetic data is composed of direct physical sensations, not ideas, judgments, opinions or emotions.

A person who is able to focus on the kinesthetic file is very aware of her physical sensations. She spends most of life either being aware of the sensations in her body or making sense of the world through her skin, body, nose and taste buds. At the level of process, a person who prefers her kinesthetic file gives particular clues. Take note of these clues to catch a person in the process of using this file.

Kinesthetic Clues:

- Eye Movements: Down and to your right (When you observe others, their eyes will move down and to their right.)
- Head Position: Below the horizontal, tilted to the right
- Breathing: Deep breathing, low in the stomach
- Voice Tempo: Slow tempo, long pauses
- Tone of voice: Low, deep, breathy
- Skin Color: Increased, flushed color
- Muscle Tension: Muscle relaxation; sudden, abrupt movements

Illustration: Kinesthetic Eye Accessing

Down and Right
Kinesthetic / Physical Sensations

Someone who is paying attention to the kinesthetic file may say, "I can *grasp* that," or "I can get a *handle* on it." In order to converse effectively with someone who prefers her kinesthetic file, use the following list of words while you get into your own kinesthetic file.

clumsy	support	shiver	unite	stiff	flinch
tickle	feel	penetrate	balance	twist	itch
stick	touch	jarring	resist	touch	shivers
shape	grasp	cram	twinge	backing	point
solid	tight	manipulate	ragged	life	fumble
tough	rough	shuffle	rugged	mold	cool
merge	pressure	catch	attack	stable	unbalanced
tender	roughly	take	steady	warm	shocking
throw	exhale	sharp	electric	handle	flat
grab	move	extend	fasten	soft	bend
push	shake	trudge	probe	smooth	hot
connect	absorb	massage	fall	firm	sturdy
link	stir	attach	compress	glow	reach
tackle	inhale	hard	cut	grope	
pack	creeps	cold	cutting	swell	

Included in the kinesthetic file is data on taste and smell, the olfactory and gustatory senses. Here is a list of terms for taste and smell:

taste	stick	sip
savor	inhale	palate
tang	breath	tooth
bite	sour	odor
tinge	sweet	scent
tongue	spicy	whiff
aftertaste	flavor	pungent
smell	lick	reek
essence	fume	with a nose for

As I mentioned in Chapter 7, many people confuse feelings and emotions. Emotions are composed and stored in the auditory file. The labels used to refer to an emotion, which may have a kinesthetic element but is primarily an auditory adventure, are not physical sensations anymore, but exist only through language in the auditory file. There is a simple test which will determine whether you are having a feeling or an emotion. (Examples of emotions are sadness, happiness, fear, and anger.)   The Test: Ask yourself, "Can I have the sensation in my little finger?" If you can, then it is a feeling. If you cannot feel it in your little finger, it is the result of an emotion created in your auditory file. Your little finger is never sad, angry or happy, but it does feel hot, cold or wet.

People in the United States pay the least conscious attention to their kinesthetic file. To our conscious focus, the kinesthetic file appears to be the slowest of the three files when, in fact, it is the fastest: it coordinates all the movements and sensations in our bodies faster than we can possibly focus consciousness on them. Consciousness is equipped to dwell on past events and ponder about the future, but it is less than adequate for maintaining its focus on the present. The present only takes place now and when you are comparing *now* to *then* you are not present. The appearance of slow processing of physical sensations is a limitation of consciousness rather than a limitation of the kinesthetic file. A person whose primary focus is on his kinesthetic file may appear to react and respond to the world in a slower manner than a person who focuses primarily on his visual or auditory file, but this *slowness* is an interpretation through a visual or auditory focus which cannot make *sense* of life through a kinesthetic focus. The kinesthetic file is so fast that it can feel, taste and smell everything in the present. Comparatively, the visual and auditory files are slow since they must access past representations in order to operate. Our system of language would not exist if people did not remember the meaning of its symbols and words. Our system for tasting, smelling and feeling functions when we are in the present experiencing them. You only need to be present to taste a banana; you need to dip into your stored auditory file to remember the label or name, banana. The kinesthetic file is one of creation. It creates without reference to the past or future.

In France, the kinesthetic file is much more a part of the culture than it is in the United States. Smell and taste are particularly important to the French. Americans focus primarily on the auditory file and secondarily on the visual file. Americans usually want to know "what" you ate, or "where" you ate rather than how what you ate tasted. One of the repercussions of focusing so little on the kinesthetic file is having a nation of people ignoring their bodies. Obesity, compulsive exercise, drug abuse and suicide are examples of the behaviors that result from ignoring the kinesthetic file. The small minority of people in this country who do focus consciousness primarily on their kines- thetic file are often misunderstood and misinterpreted by other people.

I recommend practicing getting in touch with your kinesthetic file. The feeling file is the key to living in the present. It is the only one of the three files that is always, or in fact *ever*, in the present. It is not accidental that your eyes and ears are small antennas for picking up data from the outside world. Your kinesthetic file uses the entire network of your nervous system and your whole body as an antenna to soak in physical sensations, smells and tastes. It is the most important file, yet it is the one most neglected by consciousness.

At the level of process, the last thing you do when you make a decision is check with your own kinesthetic file. You find out what physical sensations are associated with certain pictures or statements and make decisions based on these associations.

Imagine that you are buying a new car. Each time you look at a car, you compare it to internal pictures of other cars you have seen. The feelings (physical sensations) associated with each picture determine your judgments and opinions about the car. If you are unaware of these feelings, you will have to create some explanation as to why you prefer one car over another. The likelihood that this explanation will be accurate is very small because it will explain the result of a feeling by placing your flashlight beam on the visual or auditory file. The more you misdirect and yet trust your explanation, the less credible you become to yourself and the more fancy footwork consciousness must do to explain your behaviors. The more footwork it is doing, the less consciousness is available to attend to what is happening presently. The kinesthetic file perceives data about what is happening physically in the present. Since most people are unaware of their kinesthetic files, they are unaware of their behaviors; thus, they are more able to explain behaviors than observe them. You cannot get accurate information on your present behavior by accessing your stored visual or auditory data.

Your visual and auditory files are based on future expectations and past history, and for them, what we call present is either future or past. You can remember what you looked like and what you said last week, last year and years ago. While your kinesthetic file may have stored habitual behaviors, it does not contain stored physical sensations. Remembering what it feels like to swim in a clean spring-fed lake is not the same as feeling the wetness surround your body when you are **actually** swimming. Eating chocolate ice cream is not the same as remembering eating ice cream. Physical sensations can only be experienced in the present.

Seeing your house and thinking about seeing your house can contain identical visual data. Internal visual representations are stored more like holograms than like photographs. Just as your dreams can seem life-like and three-dimensional, the images stored in your visual file are three-dimensional. You may not consciously access your visual data this way, but as you practice the exercises in Chapter Six, this ability will increase.

A young girl was listening to the radio and she turned to her father and said, "I like the radio so much better than TV because the pictures are much brighter and more colorful." The images she constructed in her head, while listening to the radio, were much more vivid than were the external visual images created by the television.

Life is three-sensational: it is made up of pictures, sounds and feelings.

Living in the present is useful in gaining perspective over many of life's "emotional" traumas. Since the technology for being two places at once hasn't been developed to date, it is safe to state that when you are remembering a past trauma or concern, you are not in the present. Become aware of the physical sensations right now and focus on the present. . . . Feel your hands touching this book. . . . Feel the sensations of your feet contacting the floor. Feel the pressure of gravity holding you in the chair. Throwing cold water over someone is a useful method of bringing him present although it is not appropriate in every situation.

While thinking things through (i.e. running them through your internal auditory track) may seem like the best route to clarity in a situation, it is not. The result of this thinking cannot directly influence behaviors, and it is usually more entertaining than useful, even though such thought appears to be very useful consciously. Internal auditory and internal visual are never present and thus cannot directly influence the present. The key to bringing yourself present in each moment is your kinesthetic file.

If you think there is a bear behind you, your body tenses whether or not there is one. If you are constantly anticipating problems, your body is responding to the anticipation. The anticipation may be founded or unfounded, and whether real or imagined, it results in kinesthetic responses. Most people are concerned, worried and fearful enough to keep their muscles in a constant state of tension. This state requires a lot of energy and effort and results in stress and exhaustion. As you focus on the kinesthetic file, you will become able to monitor which of your muscles are tight and which ones are loose. With practice, you will learn to be aware of your muscles rather than your random thoughts and worries. You will have less stress and more energy to use constructively.

One of the keys to trusting yourself is to consciously become more fluent with the use of your kinesthetic file. The file does not require a lot of conscious focus. A little attention on it will go a long way toward keeping consciousness on track and returning you to earth.

Bill is an example of someone who puts more than a little of his conscious focus on the kinesthetic file. Bill judges life by how he feels, spending a lot of time with his eyes down and to his right. He speaks *slowly*, from the bottom of his chest. He is often misinterpreted by people as bored or thick, when actually, he is present and experiencing the physical sensations of the moment. Since words cannot accurately describe his physical sensations, he doesn't give them as much attention and is not as eloquent as Jim who makes words very important. To earn money, Bill is a successful and talented computer programmer.

•   •   •   •

Bill touches his hands together quite often, giving himself data which makes him aware of the physical sensations of his hands touching. The past and future are not of much consequence to Bill. Personal appearance and house cleaning are not a big time consumer, as Bill's idea of a neat house is one in which everything is thrown wherever it happens to fall. I bumped into him one day in front of his house. He had obviously dressed rapidly and in his haste hadn't stopped to look in a mirror. He had two large streaks of blood on his face and shaving cream under his chin and by his ear. I attempted to point the condition out to him, but he simply said, "Good Morning," and was on his way. It is not easy to have a conversation with someone who is used to accessing his kinesthetic file to the exclusion of his auditory and visual files.

It may be difficult to communicate with Bill if you are attempting to convey your ideas from your pictures and your auditory file when Bill is "lost" experiencing his physical sensations in the moment. If you think about your communication you will discover that you usually talk about what has happened or will happen. Bill is so busy experiencing what **is** happening that he is not a good communicator by the standards set by our culture. Increasing his ability to move his conscious focus between the different files will provide Bill with the ability to communicate effectively with people who are used to focusing on sounds and pictures without hindering his capacity to experience the present.

•   •   •   •

While becoming fluent in your ability to bring yourself present and access your kinesthetic file, it is useful to note again that there is not a **best** sensory access file. With practice you will return to your ability to access **all** of your sensory files. Any sensory file, accessed to the exclusion of the other two, will produce predictable behaviors and limit your flexibility. As a result, you will experience the same problems and difficulties many times without knowing what to do about them and without learning from your prior experience.

The goal of learning to focus on your files is to be able to focus on whichever file is most fitting at the moment. Flexibility in focusing on all files results in effective communication with others and within yourself. It will result in your living in the world very much as it is, responding appropriately, and altering behaviors and judgments to fit specific situations. The exercises to increase your sensory access flexibility, like anything worth learning, take time and practice.

For a minimum of one minute per day, move your eyes down and to your right, and discover your body and physical sensations. Take deep, relaxed breaths with your head tilted slightly to the right. Your hands might be touching. Focus your attention on different parts of your body, beginning with your feet and moving slowly all the way to your head. The best time to do this exercise is after you wake up, but before you get out of bed each morning. The more you practice, the more aware you will become of your kinesthetic file.

As you take a hot bath, keep your eyes down and to your right.

Feel your body right now. Are you hot, cold or warm? You may not have words associated with your feelings; however, you can experience them.

Keep your eyes closed as you explore the feel and texture of different objects using your hands and fingers; weigh the objects in your hands. Set the objects on a table and explore them with the back of your arm with your eyes closed (do not use your hands and fingers). Explore the objects with the inside of your arm. What did you notice? ... Could you make the same number of kinesthetic distinctions with the front of your arm as you made with you the back of your arm?

Clap your hands and feel them meet; discover whether you can do this while noticing only the feeling without hearing the sound.

Eat a banana while smelling orange extract. Try this with many different foods and extracts.

Find a special perfume and use it on a vacation. Put the perfume on months later and find out if it reminds you of the vacation. The smell in the present may bring back pictures and sounds from the past.

Find someone who has his eyes consistently down and to his right. Make sure it is someone who likes to be physically comfortable and who uses feeling words (physical sensations not emotions). Spend time around him and learn to do what he does.

Notice how you use the word *feeling* and restrict its use to physical sensations. Use auditory words when you are talking about emotions. Learn to distinguish between feelings and emotions. It will not matter whether you call something a feeling or an emotion as long as you distinguish what you mean. Rather than saying, "I feel angry," you might say, "I declare that I'm angry," or "I'm having a conversation about being angry."

Taste your food. For a whole meal savor every bite; eat slowly and deliberately keeping your eyes down and to the right. Notice texture and temperature as well as taste. (You may want to close your eyes to increase your ability to consciously get into your kinesthetic.)

Tighten a muscle in your leg. Loosen the muscle. Practice this with different muscles in your body. Begin each day by stretching; stretch your arms, legs and back. Don't force them; just do nice easy stretches. Watch how dogs and cats stretch and practice making similar movements.

Listed below are a few do's and do not's to be aware of when you are communicating with people who use the kinesthetic file as their primary sense:

Don't

Don't buy them fake flowers that smell like plastic.
Don't tell them long stories recited from your auditory file.
Don't give them long essay questions.

Do

Do hug them often.
Do keep the temperature as even as possible, not too hot or too cool.
Do buy them comfortable clothing.
Do bring yourself present by joining them in the kinesthetic mode
     when you are with them.

9

Observation

You meet people from time to time who also have flashlights and curiosity similar to yours. Some of these people have been in the room longer than you and some have just arrived. Usually the ones that have just arrived are enthusiastic and curious and never tire in their explorations. The ones that have been here longer have already come up with answers about why they are in the room. Some of these people will even keep their flashlights focused on very small areas and attempt to keep them in that one spot. They can only see you if you get in the way of their flashlights. The longer one of them keeps his beam in one particular place, the more threatening it becomes for him to move it.

*There are certain people who find something that they like in the room. This thing has survival seem a little more certain or at least apparently reduces the fear in never knowing what will come next. They then want to make sure that they don't lose this thing they like. They will take it with them everywhere. If they meet someone else with a similar object they will be comfortable. Of course, as soon as they **need** to have the object with them, the thought of not having it becomes a threat. Their* *future explorations are affected by their need to have the object. The object of their affection can be a thing, another person or even an idea. The more tightly they hold this object the more attention they focus on it and the less they are able to explore their surroundings.*

$\mathcal{P}$eople will use their flashlight beams differently. One person will focus on one sense and will not attend to other senses. We learn the sequence of senses and the focus of the flashlight beam in the first several years of life by watching and modeling the people around us. No two people have the same behaviors modeled for them; thus no two people have the same conscious focus and sensory awareness. It can be very useful to observe other people.

One of my grandmother's favorite pastimes was watching people walk. She continually expressed amazement at the fact that people could balance on two feet, such a precarious position. She noticed that everybody has his own walk. Some people point their feet inward and some outward at varying degrees. Some people take long steps and some shuffle with very short steps. Some people walk using their whole bodies while others just move their legs. Some people walk with such a fluid, easy motion that it appears as though they could walk forever without getting tired. Some people seem to have an awareness of their bodies while walking; others bump into things because their awareness is one step behind their bodies. By watching people walk, you can discover what a marvel it is that people can balance and move on two feet.

As you begin to bring walking back into your awareness, you may discover that you have taken it for granted. When you were learning how to walk, you probably didn't entertain the option of giving up. You kept attempting to walk until you succeeded. Anything that happened while you were learning to walk furthered the process. I wonder if you have ever commended yourself for learning such a difficult task. To this day you reap the benefits of having put forth that effort so many years ago. Congratulations!

What would life be like if you had decided that walking was just too hard to learn? Picture yourself throughout a typical day crawling instead of walking. Notice how different your day would be. In most situations, crawling isn't the most efficient mode of transportation. I think you owe yourself a debt of gratitude for your perseverance early in life.

My walk-watching grandmother also taught me that a person's walk is like a signature: you can imitate it, but you can't match it exactly. Not only did you learn this very difficult task of walking at an early age, but you developed it into something uniquely your own. With every new experience, you continue to develop and personalize the way you walk. One could even say that your walk is elegant in its precarious uniqueness.

Observing people and their walks, you will begin to realize what a mystery people are to themselves. People are often careful about what they say, but they don't pay much attention to what their walks say. Your walk is usually one of the first things you say to someone. What does your walk say? Observe other people and discover what their walks say by noticing your response to their walks. Do you want to meet them? Are they afraid, confident, or aggressive? What part of a person's body do you look at first? What part of his or her body do you continue to focus on?

By watching what people do and say, you can draw conclusions about the way people interact with themselves and other people. There are two distinct interactions that go on between people: **content** and **process**.

Content: What people think. The words people say, where they move, their explanations and reasons for what they do, and their opinions and judgments.

Process: How people think. The way people talk, how they move, their behaviors, the way they use their senses, and the way they form opinions and judgments. The flow or the dance of life.

Communication takes place between people and within themselves as both content and process. You can choose which one you pay attention to. Most of the time, people focus on content, while missing process. Focusing on content is socially acceptable and comfortable. It results in contraction of thought and the illusion of safety.

Life is a continuous process of converting waves to particles, converting the general to the specific. Consciousness can focus on the specific, but it cannot focus on the general. Consciousness cannot operate on the big picture. Process is the creation of the big picture from energy. Focusing on process is not even recognized socially despite the fact that in process lies the ability to generate behaviors. There is a difference between the way people walk and what they say about their walk. Walking is a process while talking about walking is content. Most people are completely unaware of their walks and will resist any attempt to explore them. If they have thought about walking at all, they will have reasons and explanations for the way they walk. Life is continually made up of both content and process; being able to focus on either one is fundamental to personal growth and may even be the next evolutionary step for humankind.

You can pay attention to content or process while you are participating in a conversation with someone or while you are observing someone. To observe content, you pay attention to the words that people are saying; you notice what people own, what they do to earn money, what sports they like, or what books they enjoy.

Meanwhile, process is what people do and the way they think as opposed to what they are thinking. Content is what they think; process is how they think. People have a broad range of content, but a limited number of ways that they think. If people influence **how** they think, they will influence everything **that** they think.

Learning is an example of the difference between process and content. It is a process. You can be taught how to learn or you can learn the thing itself. Learning how to learn will be useful in all contexts. Learning some specific content only allows you to know that content and does not necessarily contribute to future learning.

Through observing, you will be able to learn a lot about people and their processes, not simply their body-language, but their overall behavior. Given that most people are already quite good at observing content, I recommend that you spend more time observing people at the level of process.

Observing animals is a way to distinguish between content and process. Animals only have process. If you observe content in animals, it is you adding the content. If you see your dog loving a ball or your cat not liking her food, the love for the ball and the attitude toward the food are added by you. The dog has a particular relationship with the ball, but we cannot know the content of the dog's consciousness, if indeed the dog has a consciousness. We have a tendency to attribute the focus of our consciousness to other people and to animals, which may be an entertaining pastime, but it probably won't contribute to the quality of our lives. It leads us to inaccurate opinions and judgments.

One tool that will help you develop your ability to observe people is to practice communicating with them without influencing their processes. This is done by practicing being in neutral and aligning your own process and content enough so that you are able to observe theirs objectively. One way to do this is to use words that do not require them to respond from a particular file.

Unspecified Words:

think	understand
sense	wonder
guess	curious
believe	discern

When you are communicating with someone, it will be useful to ask her what she *thinks* of an idea rather than how it *sounds* to her. Asking her how it *sounds* is requesting that she use her auditory file to answer. Asking her how she *feels* about it or how it *looks* to her is requesting that she make either a kinesthetic or visual file access.

When practicing being in neutral, it is also important to pay attention to yourself at the level of process. Keep your eyes from looking in the direction of a specific sensory access point and keep your body as still as possible. This way, you will be able to observe the other person's process and minimize contaminating the conversation with your own processes.

Another way to be in neutral is to observe what is happening without wanting a particular outcome. When you ask someone a question, it is important to allow him to give you an answer without influencing him.

Here is an example of someone influencing the outcome of a conversation: An insurance salesman asks, "Do you want to provide for your children even after you are gone?" while vigorously nodding his head up and down. Then he says, "You wouldn't want to see your spouse in a desolate position, would you?" while he shakes his head back and forth, leaving you no choice but to agree with him. He closes the sale by saying, "You need to buy $500,000.00 of life insurance then don't you?" as he smiles and nods his head up and down.

Contaminating the process of others by showing them what their answers should be or by requiring them to answer using a particular sensory file interferes with human communication. It interferes with people's ability to process information and often results in discomfort and a lack of respect between people. To discover someone's processes, it is important that you learn to set yours to the side momentarily. This is a matter of having respect for that person. **Communication is only possible between equals.** One way to contribute to equality is to develop the ability to focus on and influence your own processes. Before you can effectively be in neutral, you must have observed your own process enough to know what you are presenting.

The best long-term rapport builder is competence, which does not exist in the realm of content, only in the realm of process. Reading this book will bring process into your awareness. Once you become aware of your processes, you then have the option to alter them, choose them and explore your competence in the arena of process. Beginning to be aware of the difference between content and process is as easy as observing the difference between what you say and what you do. You probably already pay attention to what you **say**; now it is time to practice focusing on what you **do**. It is also time to pay attention to what other people do.

Matching

By going beyond observing people's behaviors to matching them you can discover their processes. You can even discover what and how they are thinking. You can also practice matching yourself. You take on different postures, gestures and sensory file accesses depending on your mood or disposition. By learning what processes you go through when you are in a "good" mood, you can match those processes and return to a "good" mood anytime. Simply by matching another person's processes, you will alter and increase the flexibility of your own focus of consciousness.

Isn't it amazing that when you take on a different walk, you take on different thoughts, too? At any moment in time, you have your external behavior, your thoughts, and your physical sensations. When you change your external behavior, as you do when you match another's walk, you also change your thoughts and your physical sensations. When you change your external behavior, your thoughts or your physical sensations, the others will change too. You have certain body positions that you exhibit when you are angry. If you alter these body positions, you influence the process that produced your anger. You will use different senses and alter your flashlight beam focus. Developing your ability to alter your focus of consciousness results in being able to control your disposition. To begin practicing flexibility of conscious focus, it is useful to match the processes of other people.

At the level of process, match the body posture and position of people. If someone scratches his heads, you scratch your head. If he leans to the left, you lean to the left. If he coughs and touches his ear, you clear your throat and put your hand somewhere around your head. You don't need to match him exactly, as long as you do something similar. When you begin matching people, you will become more aware of your own behaviors. This procedure may be a bit awkward at first since you have particular body positions, voice tones and postures that you perform consistently. You will be varying your normal patterns and may have unique experiences. You will also become the observer both of your behavior and of other people's behaviors. You will learn a lot about people by trying on their behaviors, and they will be more at ease and comfortable around you. Matching someone's behaviors is a way to say hello to them at the process level. You can do it whether you are speaking to them or not. You can match their walks or the way they are sitting. With practice, you will get more refined and subtle at matching people.

By matching people, you are also varying the use of your consciousness and probably making your focus more similar to theirs. By using senses other than those you typically rely on, you will be able to match the more subtle behaviors of other people, and thus you will be able to communicate with them more effectively. You will reduce the fearful, confrontational and boring characteristics of most relationships. With practice you will be able to closely match other people's particular models of the world. You can match their conscious focuses, their thought patterns and processes.

You have probably observed that people vary, combine and mix their use of particular senses. It is rare to find someone who will only pay attention with and use one of his five senses. You may find someone who moves his eyes upward and has his hands up, gesturing as though he is seeing pictures, but is reporting on the pictures, using words which have to do with hearing. Someone may move her eyes down and to the right when she accesses her file of feelings, but she might be using words about seeing.

You may get different information depending on whether you are observing content or process. If you are only listening to someone's words, you may be misled. For example, a person may be talking about hearing while her body is taking on the posture and gestures of someone seeing pictures. This inconsistency between content and process is called incongruity.

Incongruity: When your content and process are not consistent with each other. Confusing conscious focus with the content focused on and confusing perception with reality.

Congruity: Consistency of content and process. Knowing what sensory file you are focusing conscious awareness on and being able to move between all three sensory files.

When incongruity occurs, which is most of the time to varying degrees, we are fighting ourselves by having the content of our conscious focus out of alignment with our processes. With a disoriented conscious focus, we are likely to make mistakes, cause problems, and communicate ineffectively with ourselves and others. The more incongruent we are, the more likely it is we will live in our own world of illusion created by the misinformation incongruity produces.

This misinformation has us misread where we are. Before we can move on to further personal development, we must first discover where we are. Focusing our awareness on one or two senses or having a conflict between content and process has us make decisions about where we are that are not accurate. This creates problems for us and we continue to wrestle with those problems rather than getting on with developing our sensory focuses. When we keep enough problems around, we can be justified in continuing to solve them. By nature, any solution to one problem becomes the cause of the next problem because we use incomplete information to solve the initial problem. We take into account and consider only information and repercussions we are aware of. Repercussions we do not focus consciousness on are just as real and important as those we are aware of. One thing to do when you notice a problem or difficulty is to consult all of your senses. As you practice being flexible with your conscious focus, this will get easier. Problems only arise when there is a conflict between conscious focus and that which is outside conscious focus. By learning to be flexible and focus on all your senses, you will discover resources that will please and delight you and will have problems disappear effortlessly.

We learn a lot of incongruent patterns from other people—initially from our parents. If we are unaware of process, we focus consciously on the content we are receiving and miss the incongruity. Then we match the incongruity and mislead ourselves. Other people don't present incongruity to us intentionally. They do it through ignorance of process which is habitual. To combat this incongruity, you can develop the ability to observe process in yourself and in others. If you want to communicate effectively with people, you not only need to learn the pure forms of seeing, hearing and feeling, but also the different variations that people use so that you can match their own particular patterns of incongruity.

Incongruity is analogous to someone speaking German most of the time while sliding in some French every few words. This results in the listener hearing a combination of two languages and never being able to tell which language she is going to be hearing. When someone is speaking German mixed with a little French, it would be polite to match him and speak German with a little French back to him. When someone is focusing primarily on the visual file with a little auditory file mixed in, it is polite to match her and focus in the same way. With practice, you can learn to do this without confusing yourself.

As you complete the exercises in this book, you will begin to develop the ability to use all of your senses in their pure form. Using your senses congruently will result in a clarity of thinking and a clarity of interacting with the world which will be very rewarding. You will learn the flexibility to mix and match systems at will and return to the flexibility that you had when you were a young child absorbing information through all your senses. Returning to this flexibility requires some rigor on your part, however. Since it is not part of your habitual behavior, it requires conscious focus. It will require you to interrupt your routine, automated behaviors. It may be uncomfortable at first, but with practice, it will result in competence, rapport and satisfaction.

A child doesn't develop many routine behaviors until he is six or seven. He is generally well accepted by everyone before then. When we take our three year old daughter to a restaurant, almost everyone pays a lot of attention to her. People are open and outgoing, and they smile and laugh a lot when she is around (open, outgoing and a lot are ungrounded assessments). Perhaps people's reactions are related to the fact that our daughter, like most three year olds, is using all of her senses and she is very congruent. She is taking in everything that she can from every one of her senses and exhibiting many different behaviors. When she is around someone who focuses mostly on his visual file, she will talk about pictures and have her eyes upward. She does not seem to be aware of the fact that she is matching the other person; she just does it naturally. She does not judge people, but accepts them as they are and joins them in their world. (This a trait common only in young children and great spiritual teachers.) Our daughter continually matches other people's patterns, and like her, when you do so, you can become an effective communicator who is able to understand and be understood by most people. Communication is a combination of the processes that people exhibit and the content they discuss.

As you develop access to the sensory files that have been going undeveloped or under-developed, you will discover many rewards both in your communication with others and in your own ability to resolve problems for yourself. You will live life with ease and have few worries or concerns. You will trust yourself to come up with useful thoughts and take on the belief that everything you do is purposeful. Everything may or may not be purposeful, but it is useful to act as though it is. When you believe that every action and every circumstance you find yourself in is purposeful, you work through all of life's tangles at an incredibly fast rate.

As you develop your ability to use all five senses, you will also learn to continually generate alternative ways of reacting to situations. When you find yourself upset and when you have problems, you will be able to use all of your resources and choose freely from a number of alternatives, trusting yourself to make the right choice. You will have more of what you want in your life, and what you say will match what you do.

Observation Exercises

Observe people for at least sixteen minutes per day, not in a situation where you are forced to interact with them, but in one where you can watch them from a distance. You can do this in a mall, on a city street, at a restaurant, at an airport or anywhere you choose. Divide the sixteen minutes into two separate eight minute sessions. While you are observing, get curious about the people you are watching and perhaps listening to. You can pretend you have just arrived from another planet and are seeing these human creatures for the first time. Pretend you have been sent here to study the natives without interfering with them. Make sure you observe without filtering what you see through your belief system. The easiest way to do this is by occasionally monitoring the parts of your auditory track that judge before you are aware they are judging. One way to do this is to pretend you are not yourself while you are observing and be an unbiased observer. You may wish to make notes on what you observe; just remember that while you are making notes you are not observing. After three or four days of observing, you may begin to notice patterns of behavior repeating themselves. You may also begin to notice that people repeat certain processes habitually.

When you are observing people accessing their visual, auditory, or kinesthetic files, do not point their behaviors out to them. It is rude to say,

"Hey, Bill, I just noticed that you moved your eyes up. You just made a picture." To make people aware of something they had not been aware of is rude. Use the data from your observations to communicate with a person more effectively, but don't point it out to him. If you do see someone moving his eyes up, join him by moving your eyes up, too, and by using a few visual words.

Practicing observation of peoples use of visual, auditory and kinesthetic files is a little like milking a cow. You can use a milking stool to illustrate their use of each file.

Visual, Auditory and Kinesthetic files in and out of awareness.

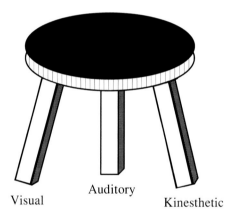

Illustration: *Milking Stool Diagram of Senses*

One leg of the milking stool represents visual data, one represents auditory data, and one represents kinesthetic data. To diagram someone who is aware of a lot of visual data, draw the visual leg of the stool long. If he is not very aware of his auditory file, draw a line so that the auditory leg is very short. If he has even less kinesthetic awareness, draw the line accordingly. Your finished milking stool diagram would look similar to the illustration on the next page:

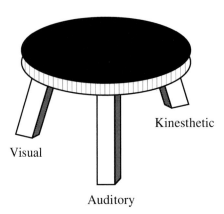

Illustration: Milking Stool Diagram of Predominant Auditory Awareness

Imagine a milking stool that has one leg much longer than the other two. To sit on it would make you uncomfortable and certainly influence your viewpoint of the world. Every time you sat down, you would be lopsided and off balance. Remember that if we diagram what comes into the brain, all of the legs would be the same length. Instead we are diagramming the present limitations of conscious focus. If someone is very aware of what she hears, a little aware of what she sees, and even less aware of her kinesthetic file, the diagram would look something like this:

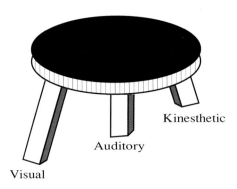

Illustration: Milking Stool Diagram of Predominant Visual Awareness

This stool is also off balance. This one closely resembles the most prevalent relationship between visual, auditory and kinesthetic conscious focus in our culture. People will have varying leg lengths, but in the United States, the auditory leg is usually the longest and the kinesthetic usually the shortest. With practice, it is possible to bring all of your senses up to the capacity of your most-used sense. Practice can result in you having legs of equal length on your sensory stool and a steady platform to live from, as you milk the most out of life.

To make these stools, you must observe the different clues that indicate the sensory focus of consciousness. With practice, you will be able to observe more clues, and your diagrams will be more accurate. The more accurately you can determine what someone is doing, the more effectively you can interact with him.

Process is neither good or bad; it just is. The more you observe process, the less you will judge and evaluate content and the more grounded assessments you will make. The more grounded assessments you make, the more time you will spend on earth. The more time you spend on earth, the more competent, satisfied and effective you will be.

Neutral Exercises

Ask three different people a redundant question, that is, a question you already know the answer to. Keep yourself in neutral while asking them. (Examples: Are those black pants? Is today the seventeenth? Do you serve pizza here?)

After you have asked your redundant questions, ask yourself:
Did you shake your head to give the answer while asking the question?
Did you match the person's behaviors before you asked your question?

Matching Exercises

Match other people's behaviors, but not so blatantly that you will be noticed. Match their breathing, their eye patterns, the speed of their speech, the way they walk, and the volume of their speech.

Practice flexibility of your own patterns by matching those of others. Once you have matched them, do anything else. Just match them to say hello to them on a process or behavioral level.

Learn different ways of walking. Find a person whose walk you like, and learn it. Try walking like a cat, but on two feet. Notice the particular behaviors and gestures practiced by the people in your life.

Try completely mismatching someone's behaviors and notice her reaction; then match her and notice her reaction.

10

Giver
Gift
Receiver

The Giver

Self

All there is.

The quantities of sensory data we perceive exist in wave form and are manifested in us through the process of converting waves to particles. The giver is all there is, and part of all there is which makes the giver possible, is the receiver.

The Gift

The Data You Receive Consciously

The data that is illuminated by our flashlight beam of awareness is a gift from the giver. We use this data to determine our worldly identity; it is so much less than all that is, but it is all that appears to consciousness. We can only be aware of what we are aware of, and we cannot be aware of what we aren't aware of.

The appropriate response to receiving a gift is to be thankful and respectful to the giver. The point of interest is that the gift is given, not what the gift is. The data you receive is a gift from the self—simply a gift and nothing more. We are in a position to take what we get and to appreciate the giver.

The Receiver

Consciousness

You have the ability to be conscious—namely, your flashlight. Your flashlight is able to receive gifts from the giver/self. You are able to manipulate your flashlight, and yet, what you perceive yourself to be is the gift (the composite of the content or process which is within the focus of the flashlight beam.) Most people do not often focus their flashlights on process so they are not able to notice much about themselves. People seldom look at themselves, and when they do, it is with a focus on content, which results in lowly materialistic opinions of themselves. It is no wonder that people often treat other people as things since that is the way they view themselves.

Through consciousness we receive the gift from the self. If we know that this data is a gift, we are more likely to acknowledge the giver and be thankful and respectful. As a gift, this data can be taken away at any time. The quality of the gift itself depends on the quality of the relationship between the receiver (consciousness) and the giver (self).

What determines the quality of your life?

The quality of your life is primarily determined by two factors: the relationship between the giver and the receiver and the relationship between the receiver and the gift. So we can focus our consciousness, the receiver, on its relationship with the giver or its relationship with the gift. In this chapter we will explore both of these relationships and how to enhance them.

The material world we perceive with our senses is not material at all. It consists of wave forms of pure energy before we process it. It becomes raw material after we process it.

Our main purpose is to process the energy into pictures, sounds and feelings. There is nothing that can be said about the energy except that it is all-encompassing—all there is. In ordinary states of consciousness we aren't aware of our contact with this energy. However, all process is the conversion of energy into form. The energy is outside of space, time and form and eludes the focus of consciousness. It does not elude who we really are, which is beings in the process of converting waves into particles.

Our secondary purpose is to dance. We dance with the flow of data received by consciousness, and we dance with the movement of consciousness. Through the dance we learn to move our flashlight beams and to develop control over the focus and awareness of our perceived world. Cognitive Harmony is the development of expertise in this dance.

Consciously, our purpose *appears* to be the continuation and exaltation of consciousness through whatever we are focusing on at the time. If we are focusing on material things, our lives will be directed toward accumulating things. If we are focusing on intellect, our lives will be directed toward learning and the thinking process itself. If we are focusing on spiritual development, our lives will be directed toward discovering process and energy.

There is nothing we need to do to be successful at our primary purpose. Process is our natural state and we engage in it every moment that we are alive. Our secondary purpose, to dance, can be difficult. Consciousness is untamed and tends to be very disrespectful. As children go through developmental stages, they often think they know a lot and that they have discovered the "right answers" to the problems of life. In these stages, they often attempt to tell their parents the "Answers" as though the parents somehow missed discovering the right answers themselves. Consciousness also goes through developmental stages in which it attempts to dictate life from its limited focus on "right answers." It continually formulates facts, truths and beliefs based on incomplete and often very small amounts of information. Through elegant dancing with consciousness, we can develop a mature relationship with process and be in harmony with all that is. The more in harmony consciousness is with self, the more fulfilling our existence will be.

Satisfying all of the demands of an immature consciousness is not possible. When consciousness is immature it tests us. It gives us every opportunity to deviate from what is really important and to chase the associations constructed by consciousness that we call reality—phantoms.

It is important to focus our flashlight beams within ourselves. This is the next frontier for humankind. To focus within, it is useful to begin observing process rather than the product of the process, which is content. Content is one step removed from process and thus is further from the source of energy. The further from energy we are, the more fragmented and divided we are. The less fragmented we are, the closer we are to our genuine natures.

Your actions continually reflect the distance you are from your genuine nature. Actions which are based on the immaturity (early developmental stages) of consciousness are doomed from the start. Actions based on your genuine nature are perfect and contribute to your wholeness. When people are in touch with there own genuine natures they will always act appropriately; when they are immature and fragmented, they will usually act poorly if left to their own devices.

To focus consciousness on process is to attend to your primary purpose. When attending to your primary purpose, you are indirectly developing your secondary purpose: the relationship between consciousness and the gift of data received by consciousness. There are several elements that contribute to the quality of this relationship as well as to the ease or dis-ease you will have in directing your conscious focus inward.

Initially you must have a fairly accurate idea of where you are. You must have practiced grounded observation enough to know where you are and what is around you. You must also know the difference between what is real and what your consciousness adds through ungrounded observations. In other words, you must be able to focus on sensory data rather than on opinions and judgments. I call this returning to earth or grounding yourself in palpable reality.

You must also be able to distinguish which sensory files your consciousness is accessing and be able to move your focus between the sensory files freely. You must know the difference between a feeling and an emotion and file data in the appropriate sensory file. I call this congruity.

Practicing congruity and practicing returning to earth are fundamental to developing your relationship between consciousness and the giver and between consciousness and the gifts received. Also important to enhancing and developing awareness of these relationships are trust, respect, and surrender.

Before I discuss trust, respect and surrender, I want to clarify one thing, which is that all of life is made up of processes. Trust, respect, and surrender are not tangible things. These are particular processes, orientations and ways of being. Trust, respect, and surrender influence the way we move our flashlight beams, our orientation toward what is illuminated in the beam, and our ways of living so that we don't bump into things that our flashlight beams are not presently focused on.

If you are in a pitch dark room, one of the first things that you might do is decide that you don't know where everything is in the room. You may decide that you are not totally in control of what is here. This is the beginning of surrender. It is very likely that you would move slowly and methodically if you found yourself completely in the dark, allowing a degree of respect for those parts of the room that are presently outside the illumination of your flashlight beam. You would begin to develop a respect for what you are not aware of and begin to trust that you will become aware of it at the appropriate time.

Where Can You Turn?

Trust

Have you ever heard someone say, "I think I'll turn in." She probably meant she was going to bed. If only she meant the word literally. If she would turn inward, she would find the only possible way to acquire the trust that provides strength. Trust breeds the kind of strength which increases the flow of human energy.

The beginning of trust is focusing continually on the process of life rather than on the content of life. To focus on the river itself rather than on the raft or, worse yet, on yourself. There is nowhere to get to in this lifetime. To think that there are certain things that must or should happen is to forget that the river will flow where it flows regardless of where you think it should flow. As you focus on process, one of the first things you must do is to tell the truth. Continue to acknowledge how things are, even when it is not comfortable for you. As you build up a history of telling the truth, you will begin to trust yourself. Trust will make respect and surrender easier. You will begin to focus on process rather than on who you perceive yourself to be.

Trust has many layers. Initially, trust requires that you discriminate between your reasons and your behaviors. As you explain, justify and defend yourself, it's possible to lose credibility and think that your explanations are accurate. Begin to notice the inaccuracies of your explanations. If you are in a situation that is uncomfortable, you might want to identify the fact that you are uncomfortable: not, "I am uncomfortable because of (some situation)," just, "I am uncomfortable." You can go further by recognizing that "uncomfortable" is a label you put on a certain physical sensation. If you begin to state sensory information as fact and all other information as opinion, you will begin to develop a history of trusting yourself. You will begin to be able to count on and genuinely trust yourself. One way to do this is to qualify your non-sensory based observations. Words like *maybe, possibly, I think, in my opinion, may* and *could* will **probably** work as qualifiers. When you use qualifiers, you identify ungrounded observations as opinions and judgments rather than facts. Qualifiers distinguish fact from fantasy and grounded assessments from ungrounded assessments.

What Are The Rules Of The Game?

Respect

Learning who is the boss is ultimately important. If you respect where it is not due, you fragment yourself and make it likely that you will continue living in a world of illusion. If you respect appropriately, you will enter into the pursuit of both competence and humility. You will learn, for the sake of learning, not to reach a particular end. You will live your life as process, bringing satisfaction to life, rather than as a sequence of content, attempting to find satisfaction.

Respect requires that you be able to distinguish between your reasonable and behavior-able parts. It also demands that you have knowledge of the tremendous amount of useful and valuable information that is outside of your conscious focus. To do otherwise is to put the cart ahead of the horse, to put consciousness ahead of self. Putting content ahead of process results in living in a world of delusion in which you have a sense of false control and false confidence. Life is a continual race between competence and confidence. Competence exists in the realm of process, while confidence is in the content realm. Confidence is based on the importance of certain content and the supremacy and control of consciousness and thoughts. Competence is a result of maintaining flexibility of conscious focus on process and the continued recognition of the limits of consciousness.

Respect is the process of embracing what you don't know yet and what you are not aware of, such as the parts of the room that your flashlight beam is not presently focused on. Respect is the process of recognizing that the aspects of your life not illuminated by your focus of consciousness determine a substantial portion of your life, even though you are not aware of them. With respect comes unconditional love of yourself, a disposition toward wonder and curiosity and knowledge to dwell on how miraculous life is. When you live respectfully you are beyond the possibility of understanding or being confused, and you live just to live. Respect is not an aspect of our reasoning. It is beyond reason and requires no evidence or explanation. Respect results in cherishing yourself independent of circumstances. It is possible to congratulate and give yourself credit for everything and to rave about yourself to yourself for no reason as you build a life based on respect.

When combined with trust, respect encompasses both what you are aware of and what is outside your conscious focus. It results in more useful and appropriate information appearing in your focus of consciousness. Your flashlight beam starts honing in on what is useful for you at the time. You expand beyond past limitations and each day becomes a celebration of the new, more competent you. This is the beginning of the process of developing respect.

Who Is The Boss?

Surrender

To surrender your opinions and judgments is an indication of strength. To hold onto your opinions and judgments takes a lot of energy and usually leaves you tired and weak. The weaker you are, the more tightly you hold, and as you do so, you lose the capacity to experience yourself, and your opinions and beliefs become all the more important. When you release the beliefs and opinions, you discover the self that was there all the time.

Surrender is the willingness to give up all of what you know for what you can learn. Surrender is also always being willing to give up your own point of view and to take on some other point of view, particularly if you are absolutely sure that your point of view is correct. I am not saying that you **should** give up your point of view. When you are certain of something, you must **be willing** to give up your point of view. You must also surrender when your judgments and opinions become facts for you. When this happens, your opinions and judgments fill your consciousness, and you are likely to miss relevant data in the present.

When a particular conscious focus is all-important to you, it is as if you have put on a pair of glasses which influences all of your perceptions of the world. You begin living in your own small world as if it really is how it appears through your glasses.

If you were to go out in a raft on a very wild river, you could frantically attempt to control your movement in the river with a paddle. You could get very tense and try to convince yourself that you are directing the raft's movements. Or you could allow yourself to be out of control and realize that you have no influence over the raft. You could make small movements with the paddle to adjust the direction you are facing—that is your disposition, but you could not influence your movement down the river. The conversion of wave to particle, called process, is much harder to control than the flow of a river.

You may as well pretend you have control, while never losing sight of the fact that you do not. When you realize that you are not in control, you can surrender. Attempting to move the raft in the direction you desire will not work and will probably wear you out. So surrender and enjoy your ride, using your consciousness and energy to influence what you are able to influence— your disposition.

Through surrender, you can discover what real power is. Power is the result of the flow of energy through process to content. At the level of content there is no power; there is only form which requires energy to sustain itself. Attention to process increases energy and power; attention to content consumes energy and power. Real power is manifested in the fact that you don't need to be in power. Needing to be in power comes from a lack of confidence and a fear that you are not actually in power. Needing to be in control comes from a fear that you are not in control. The process of surrendering returns you to your natural competence. It returns you to your natural state of limitless power. It also helps you focus your flashlight more accurately on what is valuable and useful for you. Surrender cannot be done as a ploy to return you to your power. If it is done for a reason or to some particular end, it is not surrender. Paradoxically, it must be done with total abandon and complete awareness.

•   •   •   •

Through trust, respect, and surrender, you will begin developing the process of focusing your awareness. This skill allows you to focus your flashlight beam on the areas that will be useful and wonderful at the precise time you focus on them. This skill is not conscious focusing, but what I call being charmed. You will just find yourself getting the appropriate, valuable and useful information when you need it. I imagine that you can remember being in a situation where you knew the answer to something (it was on the tip of your tongue) and yet you couldn't come up with it. Through living with trust, respect, and surrender, you will know the useful and appropriate interpretation, response, or series of processes at the appropriate time. Life will become a magical adventure, and every situation will unfold into a new opportunity for you to play and learn. You will embrace each problem as an opportunity to grow and develop. You will be able to set aside attempting to do the right or good thing and find yourself acting appropriately. Your point of view will become optional, and your range of conscious focus will become unlimited. There will be no battle to life, no resistance. Life will be a natural free flow. Using trust, respect and surrender, along with returning to earth and congruity, will make life easier and more fun, allowing you to have more of what you want. When the relationship between consciousness and process is working well, it is possible to be satisfied. In the world of content there is no real satisfaction, only the futile search for satisfaction. In the world of process, everything is satisfying. Practice the exercises at the end of this chapter to increase your ability to be trusting, to be more respectful, to surrender and to increase your Cognitive Harmony.

Exercises

Trust Exercises

Tell the truth to the best of your conscious ability. Never consciously mislead anyone. If you are not sure of something, do not act like you are sure. If you are in an area outside of your expertise, use only grounded assessments or qualifiers.

Do what you say you will do. Close the gap between words and behaviors. Pay attention to what you say you will do and have it be important for you to do what you say. If you are not sure whether or not you will do something, say you are not sure.

Decide that everyone can read your mind, and act accordingly. Imagine that you cannot have a thought without everyone knowing what that thought is. Eliminate all gossip. Never say anything to someone that you would not be willing to have everyone find out that you said.

Respect Exercises

Think about all of the things in the world that you have no apparent control over. Be out of control when you are out of control.

Clean up the place where you work and the place where you live. Keep them clean so that when you have company over, there is no cleaning to do.

Eat healthy food and do moderate exercise. Notice the conversations, pictures and feelings you have when you are eating "good" food. Notice your conversations, pictures and feelings when you are eating "bad" food.

For at least fifteen minutes, twice a day, sit or lie in a place that is quiet and in which you will not be interrupted. Focus on each of your senses for about a minute and then just let your thoughts float by in their own random way.

Take a walk: not to get somewhere, but just to walk. Notice the way your arms and legs move as you walk. As your right leg moves forward, your left shoulder moves back. As your left shoulder moves forward, your right leg moves back. This is such an elegant and purely human movement. If you had to coordinate this movement consciously, it would be impossible since there are so many muscles moving together. Celebrate your walk, your breathing, and the beating of your heart. Be impressed with the fact that you can do all of these things effortlessly. Respect yourself for these abilities. Respect yourself for no reason at all; then respect yourself just for the delight of respecting yourself.

Play some music and dance with yourself. Embrace yourself as you have always wanted to be embraced.

Live as if you are important and live as if other people are important too. Treat yourself the way you would like to treat the people who are most important to you.

Surrender Exercises

What is worth arguing about? . . . Make a list of your viewpoints and opinions which are more important to you than the people around you are. Make these viewpoints unimportant; make them important again. One way to do this is by noticing what pictures, sounds and feelings you use to create the opinions or judgments. Focus on different pictures, sounds and feelings, and the opinion will change. To tie your existence to a reason, opinion or judgment is to argue that you are much less than you really are. It is claiming that consciousness is the boss, simply because it can make up judgments and opinions.

Pick a particular opinion of yours and practice having the opposite opinion or a different opinion. Pick a charity or cause you do **not** believe in and contribute money to it.

If you are angry, upset or sad, make only grounded assessments to yourself and out loud.

When the going gets tough, consciousness has a tendency to hold onto what it knows so tightly that we lose alternatives. Make sure that you surround yourself with people you can trust so that at such times, you can listen to alternatives. Search out alternatives all the time. Ask yourself, "What other opinions or judgments could I make in this same situation?" When the going is tough—surrender. Use all of your sensory files and, when in doubt, go to your kinesthetic file. When you find yourself acting reflexively, never trust your immediate response. In such cases: When you want to be silent—talk. When you want to be alone—be around people. If you must argue—be silent. If you want to run away—move in closer.

11

Rules

There are two types of rules in this room: those which can be broken and those which cannot. Rules that can be broken are those made up by you or others in the room. Rules that cannot be broken are those that are imposed by the room. It is often hard to distinguish between the two types of rules, and the more time you spend in the room, the less clear the difference between the two becomes. This creates an element of danger for you since the consequences for breaking one type of rule are very different from the consequences for breaking the other. Breaking a rule that can be broken affects the quality of your life. If you break a rule that cannot be broken, you must leave the room.

Rule number one is that all true aspects of the room are paradoxical and cannot be manipulated. They cannot be made to serve your consciousness in any way. Accurate rules are tautologies, statements that are always true because they contain all logical alternatives and because they will consistently contradict other tautologies. Consciousness continually strives to control and use whatever it can, making the truth negotiable. However, the truth cannot be used for justification purposes; the truth just is. The fact that there is truth does not mean that you should behave in a particular way. The truth lives in "wholeness." Where everything is whole, there is no division at all, nothing to do and nowhere to get to. Where there is wholeness, nothing is meaningful or useful.

Here are some examples of the rules of the room. If the room is dark, the room is dark. If your flashlight is on, your flashlight is on. If you think you are smart, you think you are smart. If you think you are dumb, you think you are dumb. If the sun rises, the sun rises. If you like the sunrise, you like the sunrise. I could go on with this list, but I think you get the idea that these rules are not very interesting or useful to your consciousness. They must be true, though. These are the types of rules you can count on and that you can be sure of. These rules will always be true.

What consciousness perceives to be true is always harnessed into the service of itself to justify some behavior or opinion. Consciousness says, "If I can't use it, what good is it?" So consciousness has its own set of truths, its own set of rules, a fabrication constructed under conscious control. These rules can be and are broken consistently. Rules that are not tautologies lead you away from the whole and result in fragmentation and deterioration. Here are some examples of rules of consciousness: If the room is dark, I should be scared. If your flashlight is on, you are a good person. If you think you are smart, you might become overconfident. If you think you are dumb, you will not be very happy. Notice how much more interested your consciousness is in this list than the list that contains all logical possibilities. You might disagree with some of these rules, but at least you can do something with them.

If you have rules that do not contain all logical alternatives, you may often be wrong and be easily mislead by consciousness. With the possibility of being wrong enters the preference for being right. This preference provides a goal for consciousness: to be right more of the time than it is wrong. Some of the more active people strive to be right all of the time. This keeps them very busy and very active in their focus on judgements and opinions of themselves. Some people, politicians and others, attempt to have other people be right, or wrong, an activity which keeps them busy with their auditory files judging and evaluating other people. The more desperately consciousness attempts to be right, the further it moves away from tautologies, and the more it depends on its own point of view. Truth then becomes a matter of consensus. We forget our connection to our tautological and paradoxical roots and find ourselves out on the very skinny branches. From here we attempt to figure out and control everything and to find a consistent, albeit complicated, model of the world in order to make ourselves more comfortable and the world more predictable.

Breaking the rules that cannot be broken results in expulsion from the room. Among these extreme, nearly-inflexible rules is one which states that the purpose of consciousness is to perpetuate whatever it perceives life to be. This is always the purpose of consciousness, but not often perceived by consciousness to be its purpose. What consciousness perceives life to be is an infinite range of associations, (i.e. survival = looking good, survival = being right, survival = having money, survival = being married). Remember that these perceptions are based on a small amount of information gathered by the conscious mind, so they can be very far from rationality and logic.

Through his conscious ability to perceive and associate with survival, a person can back himself into a corner with his flashlight beam so that the only way to survive life is to commit suicide. Examples of this are people who set themselves on fire as a protest or people who go to war for the perpetuation of a particular ideology. In either case, death may ensue, but consciousness is focused so thoroughly on one area that it is willing to ignore all other options and associate life with the continuation of the idea. Thus, the only chance for life is to die.

The self is whole and includes everything; it is beyond all dichotomies and divisions (including life and death). Consciousness functions only in dichotomies, fragmentations and distinctions; thus, to consciousness, there is life and death. If consciousness believes in and constantly focuses on a life span of sixty years, the likelihood of living sixty years may increase. The effectiveness of the focus on sixty years will depend on the relationship between the giver (self) and the receiver (consciousness). The more effective and respectful this relationship is, the more likely it is that the focus will influence behavior. At the same time, that is not quite true since consciousness does not directly influence behavior, so it is more likely that the giver has allowed consciousness to know that sixty years is its life span. If sixty years is the wrong answer, it is probably an indication of incomplete information from the giver. Consciousness perceives that its small amount of data is accurate and complete. This perception does not make conscious data true, nor does it directly influence behavior. It does influence opinions and beliefs which are conscious events.

The better the relationship between the giver and the receiver, the more accurate and complete the information will be that consciousness receives. One paradox is that the more important it is to consciousness that the information be complete and accurate, the less likely it is that consciousness will show trust, respect, and surrender to the giver. The less trust, respect and surrender shown by consciousness, the less complete and further from the whole the information will be. The more consciousness wants to use the information (and do things with the information), the more likely it is that consciousness will focus on whatever it gets to the exclusion of all other data. To get whole and complete information, it is necessary to not need it or want it, but to just take the information when it comes, noticing it and letting it go. This is analogous to turning off the flashlight or allowing the flashlight beam to move freely wherever it will, not restricting or using it in any way. Another paradox is that to allow the flashlight free movement requires practice; it requires developing flexibility and mastering control.

Consciousness is going to make up rules. That is part of its nature. Rather than paying attention to what rules are the right ones, let's look at what rules might allow you to live a better and more enjoyable life: What rules might improve the relationship between consciousness and self? What rules will enable you to live a more respectful life with greater ease?

There are several rules that will contribute to the relationship between consciousness and self. Life will get better if you presuppose that these optional rules are true and live in accordance with them. These are rules that you can break without having to leave the room. However, you will have to pay for breaking them, and the payment is a decrease in the quality of life. As you break these rules, your quality of life goes down and may eventually reach a point where your life is not worth living.

Here are the rules:

- **The map is not the territory.**

- **The meaning of the communication is the response you elicit.**

- **If what you are doing isn't working, do anything else.**

- **If what you are doing is working, do anything else.**

- **It is useful to make a distinction between consciousness and self.**

- **The person with the most alternatives has the broadest range of contributions to make.**

- **People have all of the resources they need available to them.**

- **You always get what you want.**

Let's explore each of the rules in some depth:

- **The map is not the territory.**

This states succinctly the human plight, discussed earlier, which is that we don't ever deal with the world itself. The closest we can come to the world itself is to perceive it through our senses. We use the data from our eyes, ears and body to build our sensory grounded assessments. Eating chocolate is very different from reading about eating chocolate. Having sex is different from thinking about having sex. There is a difference between experience and thought. There is a difference between the menu and the meal. You can eat, experience and be nourished by the meal. The menu is a representation of the meal. Our senses are removed from that which we perceive. Language is a representation of what we sense, thus language is twice removed. Language is like a report on the menu. Our senses are a report on experience.

It can be useful to keep in mind that, consciously, all we have are our judgments and opinions. No matter how real we think they are, language and thoughts are still twice removed representations of the world and experience. This rule can contribute to the goal of maintaining flexibility in our thoughts and opinions. It can motivate us to use our conscious focus in different sensory files. It can allow us to keep in mind that the experience of the map is different from the experience of the territory. If a map is not accurate, it is usually a lot more difficult and time consuming to change the territory to fit the map, or to live as if the map is accurate when it is not, than to change the map.

It improves the quality of life to go on refining, adjusting, changing and being willing to throw out the map at all points in time. Quality of life can also be enhanced by observing other maps and determining which map results in your being more alive, aware and awake.

- **The meaning of the communication is the response you elicit.**

This rule puts the responsibility of communication directly on you. You are the originator of language and, as such, your job is to observe the effect of your language both on yourself and on others. You can learn to focus your flashlight beam on your own auditory files and on the behaviors of others when you speak. Other people will respond in proximity to what you say, and if you do not like their response, you can be flexible and change your language to elicit a different response. Remember that when you speak, you speak from a search of your files, and what you say, in turn, produces a search of files in your listener. To communicate, you will need to be able to notice your behaviors and those of your listeners. You must be able to alter and vary your file searches. It is your responsibility (response-ability) to interact with other people in such a way that they will be inclined to do various searches. Communication is not your fault or their fault. When communication takes place, you can influence how tightly you hold the end product of a file search by how long you keep your flashlight focused on a particular end result.

Communication is initially a no-fault event. It becomes a fault event if you keep your flashlight on the opinions and judgments you make about behaviors rather than altering the behaviors by inspiring other searches of the files. The responsibility for communication is always yours. For example, if you act as if this is true, when you request that someone stand up and he remains sitting, what you requested is that he remain sitting. This may seem a little odd at first, but remember, I'm saying that it works to act as if this is true, not that it is true. Shifting the responsibility for communication to the speaker initiates an active model of communication that holds flexibility as its foremost principle. It is possible to adjust communication continually to always get the desired result. Accepting responsibility for communication eliminates conversations that start out, "You didn't do what I told you to," or "I told you so."

At any point in time, you have what you are aware of and what you are not aware of going on within you. When you say something to someone, you probably focus consciously on the content of what you say and ignore the pictures, sounds and feelings outside your awareness. People may listen to your words, but they are also influenced by the sensory files outside your awareness. As discussed in earlier chapters about the senses, the sensory files outside of your awareness are apparent in your behaviors. Since the files you are unaware of are determining your behaviors, it makes sense that people will always respond first to the behaviors and sensory clues you convey that are out of your awareness; somehow people know that these are more trustworthy. Likewise people will usually respond to file searches you are unaware of with file searches they are unaware of. These will affect their behaviors, but not their opinions and judgments. Linguists have been saying for years that between ten and twenty percent of communication is the content of the spoken words. The other eighty to ninety percent is process or behaviors.

An example of this is in a sales situation. A salesperson can request that you buy something, and at the same time, make a picture in her head of your not buying it and have a physical sensation associated with your not buying. As far as the sales person is consciously concerned, she asked you to buy. At the same time, she conveyed to you the results of her file searches that indicated you should not buy. These types of mixed messages are very common and are a consequence of the limited focus of consciousness. Communication often breaks down at the level of consciousness.

If a parent tells a child to go to bed while making an internal picture of the child staying up and playing, the child receives both messages and has to determine which message to respond to. Consciously the child may only be aware of the words, "Go to bed," but he will also be influenced by the picture which conveys the message of staying up and playing. This places the child in a bind where he must determine what is being asked of him. Learning how to respond to these mixed messages is difficult and confusing for children and also for adults. People who do not learn to respond or live with the daily confusion of these persistent mixed messages are often considered mentally ill.

Time spent analyzing communication breakdowns is not of much value because eighty to ninety percent of a communication happens outside of awareness. It is more useful to increase your flexibility of conscious focus. Reducing the length of time you spend focusing on opinions and judgments, and increasing your ability to be flexible with your sensory focus will greatly improve your quality of communication.

- **If what you are doing isn't working, do anything else.**

This statement is geared to produce a broad range of alternatives and maximum flexibility. What is the difference between a rat and a human being? In a maze, a rat will stop going down a tunnel once the cheese has been removed; a human being will continue to go down the same tunnel forever as long as he is convinced it is the "right tunnel."

It is easy to reproduce unproductive behaviors. You have already performed them, so the behaviors are familiar to you. At least you can learn to be comfortable making the same mistake over and over again. Your errors become old friends (familiar and comfortable), reinforcing your safety and increasing the likelihood that you will repeat them. Making a mistake once is simply an error. Making the same mistake again is the beginning of a philosophy.

I remember being very proud of having reached a particular sales target when I was a stock broker. I was quite surprised when people explained to me that it was bad to reach or exceed my quota of sales because my quota would be raised and it would be harder for me to make it the following month. Reasoning like this puts the emphasis on continuing to fail so that less and less is asked of us. To some degree, this pattern of contracting comes with age. When you were young, you would tackle anything while being optimistic about the results. As you age, a certain "non-reality" appears that looks like reality. "It is more important to be safe than to grow and develop." "It is better to be a big fish in a small pond than a small fish in a big pond." Life becomes an opportunity for you to lower your expectations so that you are more likely to meet them. The culmination of this process is death, a state of no expectation and no failure. Death is a perfectly safe state of being, somewhere beyond failure.

We often learn more from our apparent failures than from our declared successes. I say apparent because if you learn a lot from an apparent failure and are more flexible and more knowledgeable as a result, the event may be a success in that it contributes to your future prospects. Remember that "failure" is an ungrounded assessment based on the limitations of your conscious focus. It is only possible to determine successes and failures when the game is over. If you are alive the game is still in progress.

If what you are doing isn't working, do anything else. That means *anything* else, not *something* else. Anything else means a behavior picked from an infinite number of available possibilities. Something else implies that you will choose from a finite number of options. As you begin to do anything else, you will probably stumble on new ways of doing things that will surprise and delight you.

• **If what you are doing is working, do anything else.**

If there is a tendency to repeat habitually non-productive behaviors, then there is also a compulsion to repeat apparently successful behaviors. The repetition of successful behaviors leads to a lack of flexibility. Repetition of behaviors independent of circumstances ultimately starves the brain, which feeds on novelty.

As I mentioned earlier, we trivialize important things day in and day out. One of the ways we do this is by making our behaviors automatic, doing things the same way over and over and over again. When I ask a group of people which hand they brush their teeth with, I usually have about eighty percent who use their right hands and about twenty percent who use their left hands. Occasionally someone will say that she switches hands. Brushing your teeth with the same hand everyday may seem like a trivial habit, yet it is a symbol of something important. The brain feeds on novelty and change. To the brain, satisfaction equals new and novel behaviors. And yet we make our behavior as habitual as possible, which robs us of satisfaction and vitality.

If you can brush your teeth well with your right hand, try brushing with your left hand. It will probably be a little awkward at first, but if you play the game of adding novelty by adding new thoughts and behaviors, your tooth brushing will have gone beyond clean teeth to creating increased awareness and flexibility. Brushing your teeth is only one example. Here are some other ideas: change which ear you hold the telephone to, which hand you eat with, which shoe you put on first and what route you take to work. Keep coming up with new and different ways to do things and you will not only eliminate boredom, you will add creativity and maybe even longevity to your life.

If you know a way to do something that will work, try other ways. You can always return to the one that works. In your explorations, you may discover new methods that are better than those you have used before. You may discover new thoughts and behaviors that will help in other areas of your life. At the very least, you will be nourishing your brain. When you repeat the same successful actions, you increase the likelihood that you will try using the same actions elsewhere. You probably won't learn much or increase your future range of actions or possibilities. If you are in a particularly important situation, you may want to do what has worked before. Start adding alternatives and different solutions when the situation is not important. Over time you will discover that **as the going gets tough, you get what you've practiced.** If you have found something that works, do anything else. This places the process of learning and growing ahead of the content of achieving a specific result, making life a process of expansion.

• It is useful to make a distinction between consciousness and self.

You have your conscious focus and you have everything that is outside your focus of consciousness. Behaviors are generated by the self while opinions and judgments are generated by the focus of consciousness. The self is the self and behaviors are behaviors. We start out teaching a young child that if she does something "good," then she is a good girl. So we begin to associate that if we do "good" things we are good people and if we do "bad" things we are bad people. We learn to try to do "good" things to be good people. If, in the midst of doing "good" things, we do something "bad", we fear that we may become bad people. Your consciousness will continue to judge people's behaviors as "good" and "bad." Your consciousness can, however, learn to distinguish between behavior and the person who is behaving.

Beliefs have a way of determining perceptions. When we decide that someone is a bad person, in addition to the decision being ungrounded as a result of making the judgment, we expect him to do "bad" deeds. And, of course, he acts badly since that is what we are looking for. As Abraham Lincoln said, "If you look for the bad in people expecting to find it, you surely will." We focus our consciousness mostly on the "bad" deeds and seldom on the "good" ones. If we say we don't like a particular behavior, the statement differentiates between the person and the behavior; thus it does not necessarily color our future judgments. If we judge that *someone is bad,* the statement influences our judgments of the person and all of his behaviors. Since we are going to make ungrounded assessments, we may as well make them as limited as possible. Distinguishing between yourself and your behaviors allows you to maintain the delightful pictures of yourself in your visual file, independent of your judgments and opinions about your actions or circumstances which are in your auditory file.

Self esteem is determined primarily by the pictures you have of yourself in your visual file. These pictures are independent of behaviors, and to act as if they are not is to have your self esteem be dependent on the circumstances and your surroundings. When dependence of self esteem on circumstances is carried to extremes, the dependence can have your pictures be different on a rainy day than on a sunny day, resulting in your liking yourself more when the weather is sunny and warm and having a lower opinion of yourself when the weather is lousy. Associating your behaviors with your level of self esteem can result in your disliking yourself if you do not perform up to certain standards you have consciously set for yourself. This is a form of self abuse that generally results in unhappiness and decreased performance in the future. Self esteem is based on the existence of trust, respect and surrender generated from within, not on the external behaviors and circumstances which consciousness judges and evaluates. A brain surgeon who operates on herself has a fool for a patient. A person who pays much attention or lends much credibility to her subjective opinions of herself is acting foolishly. Remember: the behavior is the behavior and a judgment about the behavior is a judgment about the behavior. To jump from judgments about behaviors to judgments about the person will lead you away from observations made on earth to creations made from your world of illusion.

• The person with the most alternatives has the broadest range of contributions to make.

The more flexibility you have in your thinking, the better your quality of life will be. If you can learn to think the unthinkable, your life will be even better. The more you keep your consciousness focused on one spot or in one small area, the less flexibility you will have. Restricting your focus of awareness is like being in a cage. The size of the cage is determined by your willingness to move your conscious focus. It is possible to make the cage so small that you can hardly move or live in it. The larger your cage, the better your life. By continuing to vary your focus of consciousness and not allowing yourself to become addicted to a specific focus, it is possible to let yourself out of the cage completely, free from conscious restriction and flexible in all areas. Becoming entirely flexible will mean even being flexible in your flexibility which will result in some non-flexibility.

It is always better to have many alternatives than to restrict your options. Think back to when you had a problem that you resolved very rapidly. It is very likely that you perceived that you had at least two possible solutions. The way we get backed into a corner and think we have no way out is by focusing solely on one alternative, resulting in a situation that leaves us unaware of the other available choices. Becoming aware of even one additional option can get us out of a corner. Having unlimited alternatives allows us to glide effortlessly through life. Some people think they have so many alternatives that they are overwhelmed. In such cases, it can be useful to add the alternative of limiting alternatives, or trusting yourself to choose the most appropriate alternative.

Part of our birthright as people is our ability to vary conscious focus, which allows us to freely alter our judgments and opinions about anything and flow through life with ease. Dignity and flexibility go hand in hand, in that dignity represents who you really are: a self with all alternatives available to you. Dignity is a view of self as unlimited. Limitations are imposed by consciousness without consideration of self. There is no dignity in consciousness. You give up dignity when you focus on consciousness as self.

Nobody can limit your alternatives but you. You are the master of your perceptions and judgments and opinions.

• **People have all of the resources they need available to them.**

You are endowed at birth with all the resources you need for your entire lifetime. Thus, life becomes an adventure of finding your resources or finding the proper nurturing to discover all of the resources you possess. If you think you are missing some of your resources, then you are somehow deficient or broken and must try to find someone or something outside yourself to give you the resources you lack.

In the courses I lead, I assume that people are infinitely resourceful, and they continually find resources that they didn't know they had. Assuming resourcefulness allows people to learn very rapidly and puts them on the same level, where they are all infinitely resourceful. Communication only takes place between equals. This rule allows me to be a catalyst with people, bringing out new and exciting resources that they already possess but didn't know how to use. There are some people who are more ingenious at hiding their resources from themselves than are other people. The more resources you find, the more resourceful your consciousness will be. It is an ungrounded assessment to say that people are infinitely resourceful, but it is a useful one to make. This rule will have you continually focus on people's resourcefulness.

• **You always get what you want.**

That may sound strange since we have learned to use the word *want* to represent something we don't have. Thus, every time we say *want* we must inherently think less of ourselves and assume that we are somehow presently not competent to get something. This undermines the relationship between self and consciousness. It is an attempt by consciousness to dictate behavior, but it is ill-fated since consciousness cannot dictate behavior.

Saying you *want* something you don't have leads you away from the present and thus away from earth. Built into "I want" is a presupposition that somehow things will be different and better when you get it. This is your way of saying that right now is not as important as it could be or will be when you get what you want. Saying this leads to ignoring process in the present and continually picturing and talking to yourself about what you want. The present moment becomes unimportant because you do not yet have what you want. Life is only made up of present moments, so the only way to increase the likelihood of a certain future is to behave in a particular way in the present. The more time you spend attending to the present, the more effective and competent you will be, and the better your future will be.

I suggest that you use *wants* to identify what you have. To determine what you *want,* look around and discover what you have. If you have an old car, say, "I *want* an old car." If you are single, say, "I *want* to be single." If you are married, say, "I *want* to be married." You can always find out what you *want* by noticing what you have. You may notice that, at first, it will be unusual to use *want* in this new way, but with practice you will notice that it makes you more comfortable, more relaxed, and happier. Using *want* to describe what you have will allow you to live in the present more often. In the present, you have the ability to be happy and comfortable. Defining *want* as what you have right now will paradoxically also increase the likelihood of specific future beneficial behaviors and results.

If you are waiting to enjoy your car until you get a new one, you will not fully experience or enjoy the one you have. This attitude makes the new car more important than the one you have. You end up dwelling on what is not, and it is likely that soon after you get a new car, you will go through the same process with the new one. This process robs you of the experience of enjoying your car. *Want* what you have and not only will your life be more delightful, but you will increase your future possibilities. You will bridge the gap between language and behaviors.

Remember: I am not saying that these rules are true; I am saying that they will affect your quality of life by influencing your judgments and opinions about consciousness. With practice they will become part of the basic disposition that you bring to all aspects of life.

Review the list of rules twice daily. On the first day, make sure you are clear about what the first rule means, and throughout the day, do your best to act as if the first rule is true. Notice how your behavior changes. On the second day, do the same as the exercise above with the second rule; continue through the whole list of rules. The more rigorous you are about applying each rule daily, the more valuable this exercise will be for you. Keep the rule in mind all day long, continue to ponder it, and think it and behave in accordance with it.

What is important to you? . . . What results do you produce by having that be important to you? . . . What would your life be like if that was not important to you?

Make a list of the rules you live by. . . . Interact with your own list of rules as arbitrary. . . . If they work for you, keep them; if not, throw them out. . . . Ascertain where you got your rules. Were they imposed on you from the outside or did you create them yourself from within? . . . What do your rules justify? . . . Hate your rules. . . . Be ambivalent toward them. . . . Now, love your rules and notice your relationship to them.

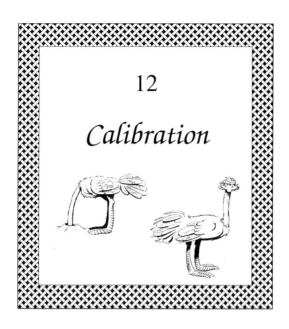

12

Calibration

The second way of knowing what is in the room is to simply trust that you know what is here. This type of knowing is not like the flashlight in that it seems much less tangible. All-encompassing trust is more uncomfortable than one little point of certainty, which the flashlight provides within a very limited context. Knowing by way of trust allows complete knowing of everything. To trust seems opposed to reason and logic, and the more you depend on your flashlight the more difficult this second way of knowing becomes.

Some people seem to be more clever, more creative and happier than others. Some people get wiser as they age, while others get more rigid and inflexible. These differences are not a mystery; they are differences in mobility and perception of the focus of consciousness. The more flexible and varied the focus of consciousness, the wiser, more clever and creative people will be.

*C*alibration is a refined type of observation which allows you to develop expertise in converting ungrounded assessments into grounded assessments.

People who are experts at calibration can outperform lie detectors in determining whether or not someone is telling the truth by using their ability to just know something. When calibrating, they decrease their reliance on their flashlights. Calibration requires trust, respect and surrender.

Just as it is possible to determine whether someone is consciously focusing on pictures, sounds and feelings, it is also possible to determine whether the pictures, sounds and feelings are inside or outside his awareness. Lying happens when consciousness is reporting on one picture, sound or feeling while a contrary picture, sound or feeling is concealed from consciousness. This contradictory sensory data results in noticeable and observable behaviors which, when calibrated, can be stated in grounded assessments. These behaviors are a result of the incongruity between what is in consciousness and what is outside it. The behaviors can be as blatant as a shaking "no" of the head while saying "yes" verbally, and as subtle as a slight change of skin color or a tightening of jaw muscles. The whole body reflects what is going on in the brain. For every thought in the brain there are corresponding responses in the body. Every thought gains reality by producing a behavior in the body. A trained observer can detect these responses. These observations are most accurate when a baseline behavior is calibrated so that the observer can make a comparison. You can do this by simply asking a question that you know the answer to, identifying the response as the baseline, and using that baseline for comparison to other responses throughout an interaction.

The most effective way to calibrate is by using all of your brain's functions. Consciousness cannot calibrate effectively since it is limited to such a small focus. Calibration is best done without your flashlight. A paradox of life is that you already know everything while consciously you don't know that you know much. The more you can move your conscious focus between sensory files, the more likely you are to discover more of what you know. The better your relationship is between consciousness and self, the more likely it is that you will get useful data while calibrating.

Calibration of process requires much less effort than calibration of content. There is so much content that it would take forever to calibrate all of it. There are a finite number of processes, so calibrating process is much easier.

Imagine playing cards and knowing exactly what everyone at the table has in his hand. In poker, there are good hands and bad hands. Your response to an extremely good hand will be different than your response to an extremely bad hand. To be a good poker player, you must be able to look like you have a good hand when you have a bad hand and vice versa. To be effective at communication, you must look like you have a good hand when you have a good hand. A trained poker player who is good at calibration will be able to consistently know how good your hand is, and even have a good idea which cards you hold, without the use of conscious focus (concentration). Calibration requires a respectful relationship between consciousness and self.

During a course I conducted, a woman who was not a card player was confronted with the task of determining whether the person across from her had a good or a bad hand. She was accurate about fifty percent of the time. The moment she closed her eyes, she was correct one hundred percent of the time. She was astonished to discover that she just knew what type of hand the person had. With her eyes open, she was focusing her consciousness on what she was seeing and was getting mixed messages. With her eyes closed, the message became clear and simple. We are all able to just know everything, and few of us are able to know that we just know. So much of what happens in our lives reinforces the gap between consciousness and self, and the larger the gap the more likely it is that consciousness will maintain its small focus to the exclusion of knowing. The self is always accurate. The self not only knows whether someone has a good or a bad hand, it knows all of the cards in her hand.

You always know in your self precisely what will be the most appropriate behaviors, opinions and judgments for every occasion. The problem is that consciously you don't know that you know. There are many lessons that you must learn. Your consciousness is a student and the self is a teacher. The self must continually watch consciousness and give it room to do what is necessary in order to learn, grow and develop.

Consciousness is often incongruent and sometimes intentionally misleading; in other words, conscious focus often lies. Lying results when you have your flashlight on what you think is true while you are saying something different. Another word for lying is *sin*, which is an ancient archery term meaning "off the mark." There is a distinction between lying and incongruity. Incongruity often results from lying, whereas lying is always a product of incongruity. Lying is cumbersome, at best, and usually destructive. Lying is not effective in that there is a fundamental reality which consciousness cannot change. At the level of self, you know when you are lying, and so does everyone else. Lying is not possible at the level of self. Lying is a short-term solution to problems and its use results in a loss of conscious credibility.

Consciousness is off the mark often enough, even when it is doing its best. So to lie or use sarcasm, even in jest, is counterproductive.

There are two types of lies. The first is a lie which is the result of misfiled sensory data either in or out of consciousness. This kind of lying is accidental and inherent in the workings of a limited focus of consciousness. As defined in Chapter 9, I call this type of lying: **incongruity**—*when your content and process are inconsistent with each other.* The second type of lying requires full awareness and occurs as a result of having blatantly opposite thoughts within consciousness at the same time. I call this behavior: **criminal**—*lying while knowing that you are lying and doing it intentionally.*

Incongruity is often the source of misunderstanding and the inability to trust yourself. Incongruity does not mean that you cannot trust yourself; it is that you cannot trust consciousness. As a result of incongruity you often say that you cannot trust yourself, however, you can always trust yourself, and you can sometimes trust consciousness. If you mistake consciousness for self, you are providing yourself with fuel to be even more incongruent and to doubt yourself. Doubt is not knowing whether to trust consciousness or self. Consciousness is not your whole self. Learn to distrust consciousness and you will prosper. Learn to distrust your whole self and your life will not be worth living.

Every time a person lies, that person drives a wedge between consciousness and self. The wedge driven when a person is incongruent is smaller than that which is driven when a person is being criminal. Incongruity and criminal lying produce noticeable physical manifestations—observable signs on the face and body. With practice, you will learn to observe these signs and know whether you or someone else is lying and being incongruent or telling the truth and being congruent. These signs are individual and personal, so it is necessary to observe and calibrate each person.

If your consciousness does not know that someone is lying, you will be easily misled. You will continuously focus on the superficial content of his communication and not know the meaning or consequences of the communication. The larger the discrepancy between your consciousness and self, the more often you will be misled and misinterpreted. The less effective you are at calibration, the more you will appear to be a victim of other people's lies. You are really a victim of your own inability to observe and of the relationship between your consciousness and your self. The better you are at observation and calibration, the less of a victim you will be.

To be a victim is to perceive that something is outside of your control. Since everything is out of your control except your judgments and opinions, it is likely that you will often perceive yourself as the victim of circumstances or of other people. As I said earlier, your consciousness cannot directly influence your behaviors or the behaviors of another. The more your judgments and opinions are in line with the self, the more of a contribution the self makes. The bigger the gap between consciousness and self, the more of a problem and a liability consciousness becomes. To claim that you are a victim is to attempt to argue for the supremacy of consciousness over self.

If you are skilled at calibration, few people can mislead your consciousness. Someone can tell you that he will pay you a certain sum of money or that he will meet you at your house at 6:00 P.M., and you will know whether or not he will. Without calibration, you must assume he will do what he says and you can be misled easily. Once misled, you can blame other people and become indignant or angry; you can blame yourself and further decrease your self esteem. (Low self esteem is simply the focusing of consciousness on less than glorious pictures or conversations about yourself.) Neither of these alternatives produces a brighter, more effective future.

A more useful alternative is to learn calibration so that you can be misled less often and like yourself better. If you take on a victim mentality, the problem will always be with other people: they are bad and you are just their innocent victim. This judgment decreases your flexibility; while increasing flexibility is vital to being autonomous and living well. To produce evidence of victimization, a victim must be continually misled. The judgment that you are a victim results from your inability to calibrate effectively and increases the likelihood that you will continue to be a victim in the future. With enough practice in living this pattern, it is possible to become the victim of being a victim.

As with all learning, you will make your initial calibration consciously, and though it may be cumbersome, with practice you will find yourself just knowing. The more you practice calibration consciously, the better you will get at it, and the better the relationship between your consciousness and self will be.

It is ironic that when the going gets tough, we tend to immediately rely on consciousness. Focusing our energies on consciousness is throwing our resources out the window. Isn't it odd that when the going gets tough we throw out our resources? To change this practice; when the going is easy, learn to calibrate so that when the going is difficult, you will be more resourceful and ultimately more successful.

You do not need a person's permission to observe him. Calibration begins by noticing and leads to your making more refined observations. The better you become at calibration, the more often your judgments and evaluations will be grounded assessments and the more respectful you will be of everything you are not aware of.

The people you are around have certain consistent incongruities. When you spend time with them, you learn what these are and mix them with your own incongruities. Through practicing calibration, you can learn to observe and be entertained by these incongruities rather than becoming confused and affected by them. You have picked the people around you on the basis of their incongruities, and through calibration you can become consciously aware of which incongruities you are reinforcing and which ones you are interrupting. If someone is consistently aware of pictures and yet talks about feelings, you can observe this incongruity and interrupt it by talking about pictures while being aware of pictures. This will contribute to both your own and the other person's congruity. If you are unaware of the incongruity you will be unable to contribute to the other person and you will probably reinforce his incongruity in the future.

It is not an accident that people tend to repeat the same mistakes over and over. A mistake is specific content in the "wrong" place. It is content out of the appropriate context. Unless you alter the process that produces the "wrong" content, it is likely that the same process will continue. Effective learning is a matter of varying process so that content will be appropriate. Learning in the realm of content is not very fruitful and usually results in the perpetuation of opinions and judgments consistent with those already in place. Reinforcing incongruities happens when we are around people with whom we are comfortable. They reinforce, or at least do not interrupt, our file searches. By definition, your incongruities have already been reinforced enough. Continuing to reinforce them is like going to a used food store to buy your groceries. It is supporting the patterns and searches you already make and not providing challenges that result in flexibility. Your brain is consistently storing the incongruities of others for later reference. You may be consciously paying attention to content, but your brain is storing congruent and incongruent processes that will influence your behaviors. The better you are at calibration, the more effectively you will be able to determine and reinforce congruity. The more congruent you are, the better your life will be.

Most people are so busy trying to survive that they don't take the time to look at their lives. They don't observe, let alone learn to calibrate. Some people have more respectful relationships between consciousness and self than others. Congruity is always a sign and a result of a highly respectful relationship between consciousness and self. One way to improve the level of respect is to learn to calibrate so that you can determine when your congruity is increasing and when it is decreasing. Soon after your incongruity increases, you will have more difficulties and problems in your life. As you become more congruent, you will relate with yourself better, and your life will get easier and more rewarding.

Everyone has different sensory data and variations of the focus of consciousness. This variation results in an illusion of individuality and a lot of conflict and confusion. The better you are at calibrating the differences and similarities between and within people's sensory data and conscious focuses, the better you will be at the process of life. Consciousness will lose its alienation from self and will become a partner with self. As long as you have consciousness, your individuality is ensured, so you can relax and practice developing flexibility. Flexibility will reduce or eliminate confusion and conflict between consciousness and self. All problems in life arise from the inflexibility of consciousness. The inflexibility of consciousness jeopardizes the relationship of consciousness to self and undermines the quality of life.

When you find someone who does something well, you can use calibration to learn how she does it. Determine what she is focusing on consciously, and since you already have a similarity at the level of self, you can learn how she became so proficient. If you are flexible, you can then match what she does and rapidly become competent yourself. If you determine what processes and conscious focus someone is using, you can duplicate them and learn new behaviors rapidly and effectively. If you have a good employee, determine what his conscious focus is and how he uses his sensory files. Then, find or train someone to have the same focus and use of his files, and you will have another good employee. It will be easier to find someone with similar focus and process than to train just anyone. Most people have identified focus and process as who they are and are unwilling or presently unable to alter them.

The more time you spend around people, the more you will become like them. You learn from them whether you consciously want to or not. Learn calibration and you will be able to more effectively choose whom to be around and what you are learning by determining who can contribute to you and to whom you can contribute. Calibration will result in very rewarding and productive relationships. It may sound a bit contrived at first, but remember, you have already chosen your friends this way; you were simply not aware of having done so. If you were unaware of calibration, you may have chosen friends based on the survival of a limited focus of your consciousness rather than on the opportunity for expansion, flexibility and increase of possibilities which is inherent in life.

Imagine that you are a fish in a lake. Your days are spent swimming around, eating and eliminating. That is all you need to do to maintain life. To eat, though, you must be able to distinguish what is edible from what is not. One of the main ways that fish do this is by taking a potential piece of food into their mouths. They swallow it if it seems to be food and spit it out if it does not. Fish have short memories: I remember feeding a fish inedible pieces of colored plastic, and the same fish would take a piece of plastic into its mouth, spit it out and then take it in again only to spit it out again. The better a fish is at determining what is edible and what is not, the more time it can spend eating the edible and the less energy it will waste with the inedible. If this lake has a lot of people fishing on it, a fish's ability to determine edible from inedible becomes even more important. A fishing bait may look very tasty to the fish, but can quickly result in the fish *being* a tasty dinner. The better a fish is at observing the difference between a fishing bait and real food, the longer the fish will live. Fish strike a fishing bait reflexively, without thought or analysis.

People also have reflexive responses to everything. Every word, idea, situation, person or thing results in a search of past sensory files and a reflexive response. With practice in observation and calibration, you can learn what is nourishing and what is a waste of time and energy. You can learn to become a trained observer who continually distinguishes between what is real and what you create. You can learn to tell when something or someone is a contribution to you and when there are hooks waiting to catch you. A person who cannot distinguish the valuable from the worthless is a victim who must continually make the same mistakes. A fish that cannot distinguish artificial bait from real food is not a victim; it is dinner. Through calibration you can learn to distinguish real from unreal and convert ungrounded assessments to grounded assessments. This conversion is a form of alchemy based in competence.

Exercises

Ask five redundant questions of five different people. By a redundant question, I mean one that you already know the answer to. For instance, you could ask someone who is wearing black pants if his pants are brown. He will probably say, "No," and you will be able to calibrate how he looks when he is saying a congruent, "No." By calibrate I mean taking a reading of exactly how he looks, trusting yourself to observe all of the data instead of relying on your limited focus of consciousness. In the future you can recognize what a "no" looks like on that person.

Do the same exercise as above, but do it over the telephone using your auditory file: calibrate redundant questions using your auditory file. What does she sound like when she is saying, "No"?

Visual Calibration

Find a willing partner. Have him think of someone that he likes. Don't have him talk or tell you who the person is; just have him think of the person. Your job is to observe what he looks like when he is thinking about someone that he likes. Then have him move around or cough or think about ducks and tree frogs to interrupt his thinking.

Now, have him think of a person that he doesn't like. Observe what he looks like when he is thinking about that person. Then distract him by having him move around or cough or think about ducks and tree frogs. Repeat the process of having him think of the person he likes, and observe how he looks. Distract him and then have him think of the same person he doesn't like. After you have calibrated what he looks like when he thinks about someone he likes and someone he doesn't like, test your calibration. Make sure he thinks of the same people he thought of when you were calibrating him. Ask questions for which each of the answers will most likely fit one of the people, such as the following:

Which one of these two people lives closer to you?
Which one of these two people has longer hair?

Which one of these two people eats more pizza?
Which one of these two people has more shoes?
Which one of these two people wears more blue?
Which one of these two people is taller?

Your partner then thinks of one of the two people, and you get to tell him which one he is thinking of based on your calibration. Your partner will let you know if you are correct. You may need to re-calibrate if you find yourself getting some right and some wrong. If your partner doesn't know which person fits a particular question best, have him pick one anyway. If you get them all wrong, then you have calibrated perfectly—you need only give the opposite response. If you get them all right, you may want to do the exercise again and request that your partner hide some clues from you to make it more challenging. If you get some right and some wrong, you may want to do the exercise again and request that your partner give you more blatant clues. The key here is to pay attention to the whole person as you are calibrating and to trust your self to do the calibrating. If you pay attention to one or two things consciously, you may be misled. If you pay attention with your self, you will pick up many clues and always be accurate. To use self for calibration requires ignoring your conscious focus and applying the principles of trust, respect and surrender discussed earlier.

With practice, you can determine whether someone agrees with you without waiting for her response. This determination can allow you to respond to what she is really saying rather than just what she is saying consciously. Make up your own variations of the above game and become proficient at visual calibration. If you use the results of your newfound competence to attempt to manipulate people, you will be less effective in learning and using calibration.

Auditory Calibration
"The Check is in the Mail"

Find a willing partner. Close your eyes. Have your partner tell you about something she did yesterday. Notice what you notice. Calibrate how a person sounds when she is telling the truth. Make sure you keep your eyes closed or your back to her during the exercise and have your partner tell you something else she did yesterday. Then have your partner lie to you about something she did yesterday. (Have her tell you she did something yesterday that she did not do.) In this culture, we don't often request that someone lie to us. However, I have noticed that this hasn't stopped people from lying. Wouldn't life be different if you requested of people what they were going to do anyway? Again, have your partner lie to you about something she did yesterday. Calibrate how she sounds when she is lying. Now test your calibration: have her tell you about something she did yesterday, either making it up or reporting on something she did. Determine whether she is lying or telling the truth, and then say, "Tell me about something you did yesterday." Your partner either lies to you or tells you the truth. Make up your own variations of this exercise and practice calibration.

When I was a stockbroker, calibration was very important. Most of my business was conducted over the phone. When a client bought stock, particularly a new client, I had to make sure it was an order he was going to pay for. If he did not pay in five business days, I was liable for potential loss incurred by the purchase of the stock. If, over the course of five days, the stock went down, I had to pay for the loss; if it went up, the brokerage firm got the profit. Not knowing how to calibrate can be costly in all areas of life. It can cost money, friendships, marriages, business deals or almost anything.

You may want to practice this exercise often if you spend time on the phone or if you ever converse with people. The idea isn't for you to do it perfectly, but to practice making the distinctions and taking the readings. People usually don't expect themselves to play golf on a difficult course and shoot par the first time. I find that they generally do, however, expect themselves to be perfect at interpersonal interactions even though they have been practicing and habitualizing their current behaviors and patterns for twenty, thirty, forty, fifty, sixty, seventy or eighty years. Well, I have bad news for you: it takes only an instant to change, but the time leading up to a change is sometimes much longer than that.

Kinesthetic Calibration

One way to practice kinesthetic calibration is to find two willing partners. Sit opposite them within easy reach. Relax and close your eyes.

Have one of the two people touch your knee with one finger and say her name. Have the other person touch the same knee in the same place with one finger and say his name. Calibrate the touch of each of the people. Do this several more times until you know the difference in their touches.

Test your calibration by having one of them touch you while you identify which one it is. If you are accurate, she says "Yes"; if you are inaccurate, she says her name. Do this exercise until you can consistently distinguish the touches. Make up variations of this exercise to become proficient at kinesthetic calibration.

Learn to trust your kinesthetic response. None of the calibration exercises requires conscious thought. Your self already knows the right answer, so learn how to focus consciousness on the appropriate spot in your files to get the answer. This requires that you trust your ability to get the right answer and that you trust the answer you get. The more you think consciously about these exercises, the more difficult they will become. The more you trust yourself, the easier and more accurate your life will be.

You can also use calibration to determine what is happening with someone else. To do this, sit across from someone as both of you have your eyes closed. Have him think of some emotional state while you are holding his wrist. Then interrupt his emotional state by having him think of something else. Then have him think of some other emotional state as you continue to hold his wrist. Interrupt him after each emotional state. Label the first state "A" and the second state "B." Calibrate the difference between emotion "A" and emotion "B." Now have him pick either "A" or "B" and tell him which one he picked just by calibrating the sensations from his wrist. This exercise may be a little difficult at first, but with practice you will be able to do it easily. You will be able to tell what emotional state or frame of mind people are in just by being anywhere near them. You can do this same exercise by watching someone in different emotional states and learning to distinguish between the emotions. It can also be done without touching and with your eyes closed, based on people's voices.

There are infinite variations of the calibration exercises, and every interaction with another person or with yourself is an opportunity to practice calibration. Make up your own exercises and try them. Experiment and play and you will learn. This type of learning applies to all aspects of life.

12 1/2

Good and Bad

*I*magine that one day you go out for a walk (good). As you are walking, you enjoy the stretching you are doing with your body (good). But you notice that one muscle in your leg is tight (bad). As you notice the tightness, it begins to loosen and relax (good). As you walk, you notice that your brain is not stretching (bad). You raise your eyes and become aware of pictures in your head (good). When you do this, you lose awareness of your body (bad). Your brain is now being stretched, and you move to the kinesthetic posture to continue your practice (good). You want to determine how well you are doing in your kinesthetic file (good), so you move to your auditory file to judge it (bad). You notice that to judge pictures or feelings, you have to go to your auditory file (good). You find yourself dwelling in your auditory file, constantly judging yourself (bad). You remember that this is only practice, and you can move your flashlight beam between senses (good).

You are having a wonderful time on your walk (good). You just made an ungrounded assessment about the walk (bad). You notice that it is an ungrounded assessment (good). You are practicing and learning as you walk (good). You forget where you are and discover that you are lost (bad). Sure you're lost, but you learned a lot and discovered much about yourself (good). You look around and get confused (bad). The more you look around, the more your confusion turns to curiosity (good). You see a huge wall ahead of you (good). You think that the wall is in the way of the direction you should go (bad). The wall limits the number of directions you can go and thus limits your confusion (good). The more you look at the wall, the more you decide it is in the way of the only direction that is worth going (bad). You get curious about the wall (good). You decide that you must get to the other side of the wall (good). You decide that you will get to the other side of the wall (good). You decide that life will not be satisfying or worth living until you get to the other side of the wall (bad). You have no idea how to get to the other side (bad). You sort through the files in your brain and find numerous times that you have succeeded at difficult tasks (good). As you sort, you also come up with times you failed (bad). You look at the wall again and attempt to figure out how to get to the other side (good). You look at other alternatives to climbing the wall (good). You decide you must climb the wall (bad). You attempt to climb the wall (good). You make it several feet up the wall (good). You fall back down to where you started (bad). You keep trying, remembering that to be of value, something must be really difficult (dumb). You spend a lot of time attempting unsuccessfully to climb the wall (bad).

You remember that you have a friend who does mountain climbing (good). You remember that you are lost, so you do not know how to get to your friend's house (bad). You focus your consciousness back on the wall and attempt to figure out how to get to the other side. You get angry and blame the wall for your anger (bad). You settle down and notice that the wall is not very emotional (good). You noticed that two sentences back I left out good or bad (good). You expected it to be there though (bad). You had reasons and explanations for why it wasn't (bad). You begin to laugh at the wall (good). You remember that the wall might not even be there if it were not for you (good). You don't know why the wall would be put in your way (bad). You trust that there is something you have to learn from the wall (good). You want to know everything already (bad). You begin to wonder if it is really worth getting to the other side of the wall (good). It might be awful on the other side (bad). But it might be the only way home (bad). You remember that you can never really go home again because home will have changed by the time you get there (bad).

You begin to look at the wall as a challenge (good). You begin to enjoy attempting to get to the other side of the wall (good). You enjoy the very process of interacting with the wall (good). You remember that since there is nowhere to get to any road will take you there (good). You are exactly where you are (good). That's true (good). The wall disappears and you walk on, living in the moment, more flexible and more delighted (good). You have a few memories of the wall, but above all, you have the learning you received on your walk to draw on for the rest of your life (good).

Exercises

There are a number of ways to add flexibility to your life. One way is to practice making many different judgments on the same subject. An exercise you can use to practice this is to choose some common household object and make observations, judgments and opinions about the object. As an example, let's pick a dishwashing soap container. Notice that as quickly as you can read what the object is, you make a picture of it in your head. (Some people may be less aware of the picture than others). If you can see the picture, notice what shape, color and size it is. Notice all of the features of the container.

Your brain supplies you with pictures faster than you can consciously see them. One of the main jobs of consciousness is to focus on a particular picture, sound or feeling, separate and distinct from all others.

Now, get a real container of dish washing soap. Notice whether the one you get is similar to your picture of the container. Keep looking at the container of dishwashing soap and come up with a list of ten things you like and ten things you don't like about it.

Focusing on the same container of soap, think of at least ten uses for the soap, the container, or the combination of soap and container. Now think of ten different uses. Your uses don't have to be clever or have marketing potential. Just allow yourself to create new uses for the fun of creating new uses. Choose one of the new uses and decide that it is a wonderful use. Find five attributes of the wonderful use. Now imagine that the use is bad and find five negative consequences of it.

Do this same exercise with several other objects. Also, do this exercise about yourself as though you are the product.

We have a tendency to decide that people who have realities (conscious focus) similar to ours are good people and that people with realities different from ours are bad people. These tendencies exhibit themselves in such ways as who we spend time with and the quality of time we spend with them. It is ironic that flexibility is the key to interacting with other people more effectively, yet we spend time with people who are similar to ourselves, doing similar behaviors over and over again, and missing the opportunity to develop flexibility. Begin spending time with people who are very different from you to increase your flexibility. Notice the judgments and opinions you make about people. Notice the judgments and opinions you make about your comfort with different people. Determine what your comfort is based on and learn to use comfort as an indication that you should be more flexible. When you say you are uncomfortable with someone, spend more time with her while you practice flexibility, until you are comfortable. Discomfort and confusion are indicators that you are outside of habitual routine behaviors. When you are outside of habitual behaviors, your options are unlimited.

13

Wake-Up

The easiest way to be secure in this room is to stay within your own little area that you have fully explored. For this strategy to work, it is also necessary to only allow people into your area who are limiting their focus. With a little imagination, you can even decide that your area is really the whole room. You can spend your days focusing your light on familiar objects and people within your area. One problem you will have with this approach is that there will be a nagging realization that your area is not all there is and that this "security" you have developed is not so secure after all. Remember that in this room nothing is what it seems. The sense of security you develop in this room is an illusion and is really insecure.

I went to Seattle several years ago; a friend of mine picked me up at the airport. We took the elevator to where her car was parked, and on the elevator were two businessmen, a little girl, her little brother and their mother. As the elevator started to move, the little girl let out a high-pitched scream that was like the unpleasant whine of a dental drill. Everyone on the elevator tensed their bodies. This was probably not the first time the little girl had done this. It appeared that she used this sound to manipulate and control the people around her.

I joined her in the sound. I used a similar volume and pitch for just a fraction of a second. My sound was quick, but effective. The little girl stopped yelling and looked up at me. Her mother missed getting off on her floor because what had happened didn't make sense to her. My noise was just loud enough to have the girl wonder, "What is this? Don't join me on my terms. This is how I run the world. Nobody else can do this. It's mine." She continued to stare at me with apparent curiosity.

It is usually rude to interrupt someone when he is speaking. However, interrupting someone's behavior is not necessarily rude. It is impolite to let someone continue with an unproductive or destructive behavior. It is rude to let her go on negatively influencing herself or others. The little girl had been rewarded for her yell and used it to terrorize her family. I interrupted the yell which shifted the habitual patterns of interaction in the family and made it possible for other more productive patterns to emerge.

Initially, every behavior and thought is purposeful, but not always appropriate contextually or ecologically. It is always the best behavior based on the information available to the person producing the behavior. The information, however, is not always accurate and never complete. The wider the range of behaviors available to you, the more likely it is that you will act appropriately. You generate behaviors based on a search of your sensory files. The more similar one search is to another, the fewer behaviors you will have available. The fewer behaviors you have available, the more automatic and habitual your life becomes, and the less aware, awake and alert you will be. This narrowing of behavioral variety results in your reaction to one situation being like your reaction to a different situation. To consciousness, this limitation of responses seems safe. In reality, it is not safe since deciding that two situations are the same when they are, in fact, different can be quite dangerous. You lose the ability to distinguish differences, and your behaviors become rigid and predictable even though the world is neither rigid nor predictable.

The more thoroughly you can distinguish between two things, the more dissimilar your file searches will be regarding those things. If you have a doctorate in chemistry, you will have more questions and far more answers about atoms than someone who has never studied them. Knowledge results in your ability to make far more distinctions than you would otherwise be able to and in having a wider range of useful behaviors. It leads to a complexity of sensory file searches and a depth of behaviors we call expertise. Continued growth and expansion requires the continual posing of more refined questions, with each question demanding a more refined file search than the one before it.

When consciousness is focused on a question, it must continually seek answers. Questions keep consciousness awake and alert. When faced with an answer, consciousness tends to become dull and constricted. It holds to the answer and misses the results of the next file search. The more it ignores the results of the next search, the less flexible and the more rigid it becomes. Consciousness restricts its focus and misses the constant flow of data from the world. It neglects the process of wave to particle and focuses on one particle, which is never real until we process it, and then only encounters reality at the moment of processing. To continue focusing on the particle may seem a safe and comfortable course of action, but it is actually dangerous and deadly. Death is the cessation of all file searches. Life is a process of continued file searches. Quality of life depends on how varied and flexible your file searches are.

Questions threaten the tiny range of the focus of your consciousness on answers. To continue to focus on answers shrinks the size of your world. Being continually willing to set aside what you already know for what will appear next in your flashlight beam is an example of trusting yourself and the end of your worship of consciousness. This is not often comfortable, but always rewarding.

After your brain has done a file search and before it generates a behavior, it is possible for you to interrupt the behavior. When the brain is continually performing the same search over and over, you can interrupt it by changing the focus of your consciousness. All that is required for an interruption is the introduction of anything that results in a different search.

An interruption can be as simple as a loud noise that shifts your attention from your repetitious file search to the loud noise. It may be a certain smell which enters consciousness or the sight of an unfamiliar object in a familiar place. It is anything out of the ordinary that requires your brain to wake-up—to sort different files. Most of what we call entertainment is entertaining because it requires us to make different file searches from those we normally make. Much of what we call work demands repetitious file searches with little variation; when done with a variation of file searches, work becomes interesting and entertaining. Some people bring curiosity and excitement to their occupation by adding new file searches regularly.

You can think of the continued repetitious searching as a waking sleep. In real sleep, the brain goes on adventures which represent our wildest dreams. Sleep is refreshing and mandatory for people. Waking sleep is very close to death, and it requires only a slightly broader range of search than no search. One simple way to interrupt waking sleep is to require the brain to make a distinction and to search outside of its "comfortable" repetitious focus. When you ask a question with genuine curiosity, your brain will wake-up. Questions asked with genuine curiosity and anything that interrupts a sensory file search result in new and different file searches.

When I was in the grocery store recently, I saw someone I knew. He was in line in front of me, but had not seen me yet. In a negative tone of voice I said, "Get moving, will you!?" People around us, including the woman ringing up groceries, tensed and readied themselves with their attention focused on the fight or argument that might come next. The man I knew turned around rapidly and said, "Hello, Jerry." The people around us had decided by my tone of voice that there was going to be trouble, based on searches of their files. When he said hello to me, they quickly did different file searches, which resulted in their relaxing. It is amazing how fast consciousness decides that it knows what is going on, based on past and insufficient data. The initial comment of "Get moving," interrupted the file searches of both my friend and the cashier. The "Hi, Jerry," then interrupted the cashier again from the conclusions she was automatically drawing from the first statement.

The people around us did not know that we knew each other and made an immediate appraisal of the situation based on the inaccurate judgment that we were strangers. How many times a day do you think your consciousness makes inaccurate judgments? . . . The more you have to defend and protect your conscious opinions and argue for your judgments, the less you observe what is around you and the less alive you become. A sensory search can be interrupted at any time as can any human behavior.

Interruptions demand creativity, ingenuity and often bravery on your part. A behavioral interruption results in a momentary pause in your current sensory file searching: it is the pause that refreshes. This interruption makes new and different file searches possible. It appears easier to be in waking sleep and to be around others when they are in waking sleep than to be with them when they are alive and awake. It is easier to be dead than alive. In death or waking sleep, there are few options; in life there are many options. In death there are no risks, in waking sleep there are few risks and in life everything is a risk. The more flexible you are in searching your files, the more flexible you will be in focusing your consciousness; and the more willing you are to move your flashlight, the more alive you will be. The less you live in a world of your own creation, the more you are able to live each moment as it comes. Living is a matter of having your flashlight beam on the present moment. Repeating file searches many times is equivalent to focusing on either yesterday's news (the past) or tomorrow's hopes and fears (the future).

You have familiar states of waking sleep and may even identify these as who you are. A habit is an automated sequence of searches which results in waking sleep. To find out how automated people are, begin adding subtle novel behaviors to your repertoire and discover if anyone notices. For instance; put your wedding ring on your right hand, wear two slightly different socks or stockings, wear your watch on your opposite wrist, carry your shoulder bag or briefcase on the opposite side. Discover how blatant your new behaviors need to be before the people around you notice them. Adding new behaviors to your automaticity has you wake-up to your habits. As people notice some of your novel behaviors they may laugh.

Laughter is a typical response to an interruption of a normal search pattern. People laugh when they are off-balance—doing a different file search. A joke usually works well when the comedian has his audience doing a particular file sequence that the punch line interrupts. When you are outside of your typical search patterns, everything becomes possible for you, and your power and flexibility are unlimited. Being unlimited is scary, and it attacks your illusion of security in that you can then do anything, and you don't know what you will do next. Your own file searches and patterns are contrived limitations made up by you, and they can be dismantled by you.

A woman in one of my workshops said, "I don't believe that laughter means I am off-balance. I think you are mistaken." And I said, "I probably am." She laughed, indicating that she had not expected that response from me, and it threw her off-balance. Then she said, "Hmmm. I laugh a lot don't I?" I said, "Yes, you do." And in that moment she verified behaviorally that laughter was an indication that she was off-balance.

Some behaviors are more conducive to waking sleep than others. Awareness is the opposite of waking sleep and it is possible to bring awareness to the most habitual behaviors. Watching television is one of many habitual behaviors which are conducive to waking sleep. Although there is a variation of content on the screen, there is no variation of process. Television places the viewer in a trance state, by presenting a continuous variation of content with repetition of the same processes. Change in process varies all content, but variation of content can be done within the same process. The most effective interruptions take place at the level of process since changing one process changes all of the content filtered through that process.

You have habitual search patterns which result in waking sleep. The more you have used a pattern, the more practiced it is, and the more difficult it is to interrupt. I was in a cafeteria line, and the man behind me was obviously not having a very wakeful day. He was so deeply involved in a particular search pattern that he did not bring much awareness to his present surroundings. My wife turned to him and asked, "Can I borrow five bucks?" She didn't know him. He focused even more intently on the file search he was doing and did not respond to her question. Being more focused changed the way he was doing the search so he was ready when she said, "Oh, I was just kidding!" He changed his repetitious file search and began laughing and joking with her. Any variation in the waking sleep of habitual file searches holds the possibility of producing an interruption.

The opposite of interrupting someone is reinforcing her behaviors, opinions and judgments. When you are aware of the present and outside of your habitual behaviors, you can reinforce and reward people for their productive behaviors and interrupt their unproductive behaviors. You are always either interrupting or reinforcing your behaviors and those of other people. Whether you like it or not, that is the way it is. There are no time outs in life. You can never step out of life and observe it from a completely removed position; as long as your heart is beating, you are alive and participating in life. As long as your heart is beating, you are either reinforcing or interrupting behaviors in yourself and others.

Ignoring a behavior, judgment or opinion can be a reinforcement or an interruption, depending on the influence it has on people. If they want attention it is an interruption; if they want to be left alone it is reinforcement. Life is a continual juggling act in which you attempt to interrupt searches that do not further what you want and reinforce searches you consider positive. As you mature, one of the main jobs of consciousness is to assess what is of value to you so that you will be able to determine when to interrupt and when to reinforce behaviors. I suggest that you reinforce the judgments and opinions that result in increased flexibility and expansion and that you interrupt those that lead toward contraction and a smaller, less flexible conscious focus. To determine which is which, you can ascertain what opinions and judgments open more possibilities for you and which shut down possibilities. Initially this may be as simple as maintaining an acceptable level of being off-balance or out of equilibrium and learning to expand the degree of being off-balance you consider to be acceptable. As you open up more possibilities for yourself, you will be off-balance and challenged, but you will also be alive, awake and alert.

Aging usually results in a reduction of mental and physical flexibility. This isn't an inherent part of the aging process; it is the result of limited awareness and lack of variation of file searches. An alternative to aging is maturing, which gives a person an ever-increasing range of flexibility and possibilities. The more mature you are, the more flexible you are, and the more alternatives you have.

If you are reinforcing a file search, it is more likely than not that you will repeat it; interrupting it makes it less likely that you will repeat it. To determine whether it is more likely, all you have do is stay tuned and continue to observe what happens. Awareness and observation take practice and increase your flexibility. The more you are able to make grounded assessments about yourself and others, the more effectively you will be able to determine whether you are interrupting or reinforcing behaviors and the better you will be at evaluating whether you are expanding or contracting. This evaluation will contribute to your ability to spend more time expanding and reinforcing the thoughts and behaviors you want to repeat. Since life is a process and always flowing, you are either expanding or contracting. It is not possible to "stand-still."

The senses you focus on the least will be the most influential and the easiest to interrupt. Since, as a culture, we are least aware of the feeling file, the easiest interruptions for most people to use will involve touch. Touching someone will usually shift her process radically. When you reinforce productive file searches kinesthetically, you can then quite effectively bring those searches back again with a similar touch. When someone is in the middle of exhibiting unproductive behaviors, don't touch her unless you want to reinforce the file searches that coincide with the unproductive behaviors. Do **anything** to shift her state and then reinforce the shift. There are visual and auditory reinforcers; language is the most consistent auditory reinforcer. A compliment is one example of an auditory reinforcer, yelling at someone is an example of an auditory interruption. I suggest that you reinforce positive searches, in all of the sensory files and interrupt negative searches with the sensory file that is least developed. Furthermore, I suggest that you develop your ability to calibrate (Chapter 12) so that you can distinguish whether you are reinforcing or interrupting file searches by observing yourself and other people.

Most people think they want to be in glorious states all the time and be on endless wonderful productive searches of their files; they wish to be safe and comfortable at the same time. These two desires do not fit together. Striving for what you consider to be positive (happiness, joy, contentment) has you focus on future possibilities rather than how things are now. People seem to think it is their job to bring about these states in themselves and that the easiest way to do that is by having certain circumstances. They act as though when sadness, depression or anger occur, they are helpless and don't want to be in the mood they are in. Consciousness attempts to avoid focusing on negative states, but paradoxically, to know what to avoid, it must focus on them. Just as when you are told not to think of an elephant and you immediately do, if you try not to be sad, you will have to think of sadness. It is logical to consciousness that it is best to avoid negative states when, in fact, just the opposite is true. To master unsatisfactory searches you must be able to do the search without being in a negative state. Practice these negative searches and then practice interrupting them. Otherwise you will have few alternatives when you find yourself in one of these states. The way to have more happiness is to embrace and experience sadness and to approach emotions without judgment or preference. Notice what senses you use just before you are sad and use these to practice being sad.

Discover your ability to be sad anytime and, by doing so, become a master at being happy at any time. Practice focusing your flashlight beam on the pictures and qualities of the pictures you see when you are sad. What do you say to yourself during sadness and how do you say it? ... What feelings do you associate with sadness and what are the specific qualities of the physical sensations you get on these occasions? ... What processes happen right before you declare yourself sad? ... If you observe that outside circumstances determine the cause of your sadness, you will have to continually change your circumstances—an effort which can take forever and result in a lot of wasted energy. As you learn to observe process, you will be able to generate sadness, happiness or ecstasy right where you are, independent of circumstances.

Although the following exercise may not be very useful, it might be interesting. Think about what behaviors you were rewarded for when you were younger. ... Remember that you did not store realities; you merely stored sensory perceptions, judgments and opinions. The behaviors, judgments and opinions that were reinforced when you were younger are influencing you now. The easiest way to have the future be wonderful is to live well in the present. Many people think that to live in the present or have a great future they must explore their past; the logic of this escapes me, but perhaps the short exercise above will satisfy the tendency to focus on the past. Please do the exercise quickly and get on with the present.

When our daughter is crying, which doesn't happen often, we know it is purposeful. Unless she is badly hurt, which has never happened, we know that her crying just means that she is crying. When she cries, I automatically go into my sensory files and focus on all the times I have heard crying. This can put me in a negative state. To interact effectively with my daughter, in the present, I must interrupt my search and focus on what is happening now rather than what is stored in my sensory files from my past. I must be able to observe her processes now and determine whether they are ones I want to reinforce. One of the least effective things I can do is ask her why she is crying. That makes her come up with an explanation from her consciousness which will probably result in the creation of a cause and effect scenario from her less-than-resourceful state.

I must determine whether I want to reinforce or interrupt my daughter's crying or any of her behaviors, judgments, and opinions. If I don't wish to reinforce them, I must first interrupt her file search and then reinforce the interruption. If she hurts herself and I hug her, I have reinforced her for hurting herself, which is a behavior I want to interrupt. Most people "leave well enough alone" unless the child has a problem or demands attention. If a child is playing well by himself, most parents let him play and don't interfere until he isn't doing well. It is preferable to let him play independently for awhile and to reinforce his independent play periodically by rewarding him: picking him up and hugging him and then letting him return to his play. Otherwise, he will learn that in order to get picked up, he has to have things go badly. This works in the same way with an employee or spouse; to have things go better, you must reinforce behaviors, judgments and opinions you want to have happen more often. This may sound like common sense, but as you think about what you got rewarded for as a child, you will quickly discover that the times you received your parents' undivided attention were usually when you were hurt or doing something they perceived as wrong. Children learn to hurt themselves to get attention and reinforcement; as adults, they repeat behaviors that were successful earlier in life.

Time is a construct of consciousness and does not influence the searches of our files. To your brain, something that happened yesterday is no more real than something that happened a year ago or when you were two. So, if your behaviors, judgments and opinions are based on your immediate response to a file search without the perspective of the present, you will often respond or judge inappropriately and without maturity.

If I say, "I am angry," it means that I am doing a specific search of my files which has as one component — the declaration I am angry. If my wife says, "Why are you angry?" I must search my files for a likely cause of my anger. If she were to ask why I'm angry, her question would reinforce the anger and the supremacy of the conscious focus that has resulted in the declaration, "I am angry." If she pauses and says, "How long do you think it will last?" her question interrupts my search long enough for me to observe it. We influence what we observe simply by observing it.

Immaturity: Intellectual Definition - Wanting your own way most of the time (or all of the time); expecting the world and other people to fit your pictures and ideas of how they should be.

Immaturity: Behavioral Definition - Responding quickly and reflexively to a negative tone(s) or comment(s) with an automatic response followed by an explanation to justify your behavior. *(You may notice that this definition fits better for most adults than for most children.)*

Immaturity

Response

Illustration: Immaturity

Maturity: Intellectual Definition - Developing an ever greater flexibility of conscious focus and increasing your number of possible alternatives.

Maturity: Behavioral Definition - Responding to a negative tone(s) or comment(s) with a question asked with genuine curiosity.

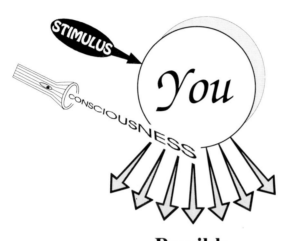

Illustration: Maturity

Everything we hear, see or feel has us go on a search of our files. A negative tone or negative comment has a person search for similar comments from her past. She will have a tendency to respond as she has in the past and will not use the resources she has developed since then. The tighter she holds to the results of searches of earlier files, the more likely it is she will respond automatically and without the resources of the present. When she responds automatically, she is reinforcing waking sleep by acting more fundamental and less resourceful than she really is. Yesterday's news may influence today, but it is never as relevant to today as is today's news. One way to alter this immediate response to a negative tone or comment is to respond with a question. You must be genuinely curious when you ask the question in order to interrupt the automated search of her files. This will take practice and will be well worth the effort. It will result in your having a broad range of alternatives when you need them the most.

The opportunity that interrupting unproductive behaviors provides is to add new behaviors to your repertoire and to the repertoires of people around you. Depending on how you use interruptions, you will be called creative or disruptive. I do not suggest that you do it to disrupt positive behaviors but, rather, to interrupt negative ones. With practice, you will become more subtle and elegant, and the people around you will have more positive experiences and fewer adverse ones. You will be able to act using **all of the resources** available to you now instead of reacting from past sensory files.

As mentioned earlier, you are always either reinforcing or interrupting your own file search or the file searches of people around you. You can't help it. By your very existence, you alter file searches of others. You are a stimulus that continually produces a response. If you are reinforcing behaviors that you don't want to occur again, you are setting yourself up for future difficulties. If you are reinforcing behaviors you want to have happen again, you are making it more likely that these behaviors will occur in the future. To reinforce a behavior or file search, focus consciousness on it. You may do so with either positive or negative assessments and still reinforce the search or behavior. When you focus conscious attention anywhere other than on the file search or behavior itself, you are doing an interruption.

You must decide what file searches or behaviors you wish to interrupt and which ones you wish to reinforce. You must then continuously attend to the focus of your consciousness and be able to have it on the searches and behaviors you want to reinforce or interrupt. Most diets focus the dieter's attention on food. This increases the likelihood of food being his focus in the future. People who have no problems with food or weight do not focus their consciousness primarily on food.

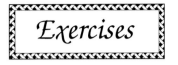

Exercises

Notice what your consciousness is focused on. Ask yourself if this is something you want to continue to focus on. If you do, continue your focus; if not, interrupt your file search or your current state. Monitor your focus throughout the day. Monitor yourself when you are delighted and pleased. Monitor yourself when you are sad or angry. Learn to continually determine whether you wish to perpetuate or interrupt your present focus of consciousness, and act accordingly. You can make this process complicated by thinking about it a lot and attempting to figure out where your focus should be. If you do so, you are increasing the likelihood that you will complicate other things in the future and attempt to find the "right answer." If you approach this process with lightness, optimism and curiosity, it is more likely that you will approach other situations in the same way.

Come up with questions about everything. Learn to doubt your consciousness. Learn to distrust certainty and to look for counter-examples, not because you have to, but just for fun.

Learn something new today. . . . Go somewhere novel today and introduce yourself to five people you have never met before.

Continually focus your attention on questions rather than answers. If you are in doubt about something, get curious about it. The more curious you are the more enjoyable and educational life will be.

Do anything in the world but watch TV for a month. That's right: No television for a month.

Practice responding to negative tones and comments with questions. Practice. . . . Practice. . . . Practice. . . . This is not easy, but it is worthwhile. To mature even faster, I recommend practicing responding to **any** tone or comment with a question. When someone says, "Hello," respond with a question. When someone comments that she likes your shoes, respond with a question that you ask with genuine curiosity. You will know if you asked your question with genuine curiosity if you are interested in her response to your question.

Find a partner. Have your partner go into a negative state. When I say state, I mean an attitude or mind set (depressed, apathetic, bored, know-it-all), some way of thinking that he isn't proud of and that he sometimes has a rough time changing on his own. It is your job to interrupt his state or bring him out of it. The key idea behind this exercise is to apply the following rules: "If what you are doing isn't working, do anything else. And, if what you did worked, discover what else will work." Repeat this exercise at least three times. (If you want find out what typical therapy is like, try to talk your partner out of his negative state. He will usually go further into it.)

During the interruption exercises, you may discover new ways to get out of a state that you normally would have had a rough time getting out of. You may discover new processes and develop competence in changing your state at will.

I got on the elevator one morning on my way to Shearson Lehman Brothers back in my three-piece-suit days. There were several people on the elevator, including a woman I had seen before. This woman usually looked serious and wore a tight, pinched expression on her face. I wanted to see her smile. There was also a young, aggressive broker on the elevator. I said, "I wonder who is going to have the most fun between the lobby and their floor." The serious woman got a huge smile on her face. I think she realized she had an opportunity to play. The young broker looked at her and then at me. I think he realized that I had gotten a response that he would have wanted from the woman. Then the broker said, "Probably you!" And he was right.

The same content brings up different responses in different people. You can practice these exercises anytime. The next time you get on the elevator, stand facing the back. Even if you are the only person on the elevator, you will probably notice different sensations in your body.

14

Time

You spend your time attempting to have each day be a little more secure than the day before it. You may even become numb to the threat of survival. As you make each day more typical and repetitious, the illusion that you can have tomorrow be the same as today grows stronger. The logic is that if you survived yesterday, then it would be good to have today be a lot like yesterday. It would also appear safer to have tomorrow be similar to today and yesterday. Thus, the more you can keep your flashlight in certain areas and not move it, the more likely it is that today will resemble yesterday. This may not sound very exciting or wonderful. It may even sound boring and uninteresting; nevertheless, you acquire a certain sense of safety from surviving.

*T*hink for a moment about real maple syrup, not the artificial kind, but the real syrup that is produced by boiling many gallons of sap which runs from the Sugar Maples in March and April. If you decided you wanted to start a new maple syrup business, you would have to wait a while before you sampled your first batch. If you plant a maple tree today, it will be about eighteen years before you can tap it. Five years after that you will be able to place a second tap on the tree. The first five years are crucial for the young tree. If the weather is not just right, it is likely that you will lose your trees and have to start over. Even if the trees make it through the first five years, you will then have another thirteen years to wait to enjoy the syrup.

Generally, we want everything to happen very rapidly in life. "Anything worth doing is worth doing fast. The sooner you can get something done, the better." The gap between how fast you want everything to happen and how fast it does happen presents problems for you. Dinner used to be a process that took hours to fix and eat; now people complain if they have to wait for two minutes at the drive-up window of a fast food restaurant.

If you say you wish something would happen that hasn't happened, your wish is in conflict with reality. This is when consciousness says it will not be satisfied until you get what you want and forgets to be satisfied now. One of the things you forget is that you only have *now*. Even later, it will still be now. When you make satisfaction dependent on something that has not yet happened, you live in a gap between now and the future. In this gap there is no life, only waiting, which is very safe. If you are waiting, you do not have to commit yourself to much because you are already doing something— waiting. **When** the big deal goes through, **when** you get the new car, **when** the financing goes through, **when** you get married, **when** you get divorced, **when** you graduate, or **when** you get the employment you want, **THEN** life can begin in earnest and you can stop waiting.

Living in this gap is usually the result of attempting to get satisfaction from outside yourself, from some thing or some circumstance. This makes you a victim of circumstances, and as such, you must search for satisfaction hoping that you find it. You operate this way because you believe that there is somewhere to get to that will be better than where you are now and that life will really begin when you get there. You put life off by making a picture of what you want and saying to yourself that you want it. You then often focus on the picture of what you want, to the exclusion of what you have. What you have becomes a reminder that you don't yet have what you want. You don't want to be reminded, so you ignore the moment and, at the same time, ignore your kinesthetic files which are always present.

Being logical about basing satisfaction on future circumstances produces an illogical result. As I mentioned earlier, if you say you will be satisfied when something happens or when you attain some special goal, then life will get better when you attain even bigger and better goals. The pursuit of such attainment leads to a long string of bigger attainments and goals, each more important than the previous one and all of them worth postponing satisfaction for. This process logically leads you to your ultimate goal, which is always the same: the final goal of consciousness is to postpone satisfaction until you die. It is tremendously likely that your consciousness will finally die. Attaching your satisfaction to circumstances ultimately makes the death of consciousness your final goal. Thus you can put a picture of yourself in the coffin on your refrigerator in an attempt to hasten you toward your final goal, that which you are suspending your satisfaction for. This goal-oriented approach treats content as important and is an attempt to accumulate the right content while attaching satisfaction to the attainment of content. Goal setting limits flexibility and alternatives while postponing life to some later time.

Illustration: Goal Setting

Goal setting limits alternatives and does not directly influence behaviors.

An alternative to this approach of being in the gap is bringing satisfaction to life rather than attempting to get it from life. Life as a process is vital, alive and ever-changing. As you enjoy the process, you will never be waiting because the process is always ongoing. You can enjoy and be satisfied regardless of the circumstances. You can enjoy every moment before you get your new car and every moment after you get it. Process is ever present, so if you attach your satisfaction to process, you will always be satisfied.

When you are satisfied, you have an unlimited number of alternatives available to you. When you must have a specific outcome, you are limited. Death is the ultimate limit to flexibility and alternatives. Life is the continuing offer of more alternatives and greater flexibility. Death is safe: once you are dead you have no other alternatives and there are no further threats. Life is not safe since it is a constant risk and it is scary. The more life you have, the less stable, secure, and certain you will be. Death is certain, life is not. Engage in the process of life and everything becomes possible for you. One way to do this is to focus consciousness on all of your senses, in particular the kinesthetic. Focusing on the kinesthetic will return you to the present which is the most efficient time to monitor behaviors so that you behave appropriately. You can only do things in the present; the future and the past are illusions created by consciousness.

All life and all existence is in process. You will not be the same in 100 years as you are now. A rock will not be the same, nor will your car, a tree, the earth, the universe, your job, your bank account or anything else. Everything is in process. The speed of the process is different for different things. Seven years old is too old for a head of lettuce, old for a mouse, young for a human or a maple tree, and very young for a mountain. To your brain, there is no such thing as time; there is just a continuation of process. If you tie your process to a car, it is likely that you will have to spend a lot of time or money attempting to get the car and then keeping it in good condition. Without a lot of attention, the car will disintegrate and degenerate faster than you do. Very few people have one car or one job or one house for their entire lives. The illusion of time is entirely relative, depending upon who and what you are.

Consciousness creates time and then becomes a victim to its own creation. As a conscious construct, time dies with consciousness; consciousness anticipates the moment when time will run out, the end of its own existence. For young children there is no death; they live every moment with curiosity and the desire for exploration. All too soon, consciousness creates time and, with it, the fear of death. This fear hampers our natural state of curiosity and exploration. The more fear hampers our natural state, the more our lives resemble death. The more life resembles death, the less there is to lose from death and, thus, the safer we are: not satisfied, not happy, but safe. The natural drift of consciousness is toward safety. Consciousness wants assurance of its continued existence and will move closer and closer to death if it thinks this movement will ensure what it has equated with life.

One of the biggest problems with life is that it is too long. Another big problem is that life is too short. Think of what you would do if you had only one more day to live. I doubt you would procrastinate or put anything off. I imagine you would do exactly what is important to you and live every moment to the maximum. You would probably not care how you looked or what other people thought of you. You would probably want to spend time with people who are special to you and make sure that you spent your time well, saying what you want to say rather than settling for what you think someone wants to hear.

If you had a week to live, life would become a little less urgent. Maybe Monday morning would still be a bad morning for you. If it were your last, however, I think you would make it your best. If you had a year to live, you would still probably be able to put things off and not live to the fullest.

How long are you going to live? It is likely that you don't know; notice that you live life as though it has a specific length. Some people think and act as if they are going to live forever. Some have enough time to tackle huge projects. Others don't have to do much now since they have unlimited time. Consciousness will live until it dies. Until then it can be vital, alive and expansive. Process is life; content is the result of living and a distraction from the process of life.

Content disintegrates, decomposes and ultimately falls to dust. The process of process is ongoing and never-ending. Tie yourself to content and you will be somewhat stable but decomposing. Tie yourself to process and you will be living and growing. Process is always a moment-to-moment phenomenon.

If you owned a store, you could change the content of the price tags on units of an item. The larger the quantity of this item you have to change, the more time it will take you. If you change the machine that makes labels, you have changed the process of labeling. This modification in the process of labeling will influence the content of all future labels.

In life, consciousness must label everything. Its constant job is to make sense of every circumstance and every situation by labeling events through language. It takes time and energy to change the conscious label you have put on any circumstance or thing, and the new labels would only be content changes. If consciousness is only focusing on content, you will have to change or apply labels individually to every circumstance. There are an infinite number of things and circumstances. To label using content will take forever, and you may die with much left yet unlabeled.

Changing the process of labeling requires consciousness to focus on process and influences all future content. Thus, using process requires a limited amount of time and has a much larger influence. Labels are ungrounded or grounded assessments created by consciousness. The conscious acts of labeling events and circumstances and knowing the difference between grounded and ungrounded assessments determine the quality of life. Making or changing each label individually will keep people so busy with the quantity of life that they will never get to the quality of life. Living longer will only mean having more time, not more quality time. Quality time is time with conscious focus on process. Process is the flow of life which goes on each and every moment. The more you focus on the content that is flowing, the busier you will be labeling and attempting to influence everything that flows by. The more you focus on the flow of life, the more alive you will be.

Focusing on process allows you to experience life itself. Focusing on content makes for a busy life in which you constantly attempt to change and apply labels. Process is forever; content is fleeting. Tying life to content is like fastening a boat to a small floating log; the boat appears to be tied down, but it is only an illusion of security since the log is not permanently attached: life connected to process is like anchoring the boat securely in place. Process is always present; content is always just passing through. Process is the constant flow of content and only appears real to consciousness when you are focusing on it. Process generates energy; content consumes energy. If you focus on content, you will age and become less alive over time. If you focus on process, you will become more alive and more vital over the years. Process is real; content is an illusion. Content is the substance of consciousness which creates the delusion that content is real and that process is the illusion.

Even though you have stored all of your sensory perceptions and all of your judgments and opinions, the only time you can access these files is in the present. Whether you like it or not, all you have is right now. To your brain, everything is present. Process is always NOW. Your body is always engaged in the result of your file search now. The content may appear to be past, present or future but if you don't experience, remember or create it now, it does not exist. You can only make a picture, sound or feeling right now. You can only remember a picture, sound or feeling right now.

People spend much of their time either worrying about what may happen or dwelling on what has happened. People go back to less than glorious experiences and relive them in the present, in order to help their future. Remember that less than glorious is an ungrounded assessment. Your stored files are only pictures and sounds that were influenced by your judgments and opinions at the time they were filed away. You do not store events; you just store perceptions gathered by your senses and limited by your conscious perspective. Reliving negative events from the past is reinforcing ungrounded assessments. History is not necessarily a true account, but something that is created or relived in the present and influenced each time it is recreated. Perhaps it is possible to recreate your history on purpose.

Think of something wonderful. Focus on something that has happened to you that you really liked or that turned out much better than you expected. What would happen if you continually dwelled on those delightful experiences? Regardless of circumstances, you would continue to have delightful thoughts. What would happen if you were haunted by wonderful memories of the past and wonderful possibilities for the future? Imagine that everything you did gave you more evidence that you really are the luckiest, most blessed person alive. Think about finding yourself prolonging wonderful experiences and having no negative experiences.

You may notice some discomfort of disorientation after you've focused on only the wonderful stored events. You may say to yourself that this is the world of a dreamer, not reality. However, reality for you is whatever you continue to focus your consciousness on. If you focus on negative conversations, pictures and feelings, your reality will be less than glorious. If your flashlight beam is focused on wonderful experiences, your reality will be glorious. If your conscious focus takes you outside the cycle of good/bad or right/wrong, you become very powerful and begin focusing on quality of life. The labels good, bad, right and wrong are judgments and opinions based on the very small focus of consciousness. They are, at best, inaccurate and usually detrimental. They are usually identified with who you are, they take a lot of energy to maintain, and they can justify any behavior or action. These labels continually influence perceptions and rob you of the present. This cycle turns into a pursuit of finding evidence for judgments and opinions made in the past while attempting to focus solely on certain content and disregarding any content that does not support your judgments and opinions. You stay fixed in particular file searches which maintain the opinions. When you consider yourself to be your opinions, you equate the survival of opinions and judgments with your physical survival. Life becomes an argument for your particular limited focus.

Life based on survival of your opinions isn't life; it is death. If you leave a movie projector in one spot on the film it will burn up the film. If you continually focus your consciousness on one group of judgments and opinions, it is more likely that you will burn up your life, allowing that particular content to triumph. A conversation about quality of life with someone who is constantly expending energy to support the "illusions" of life is not useful or relevant.

Time is created, maintained, and manipulated by consciousness. When we have a problem, we generally think it will last forever. When we have something wonderful happen, we think it is fleeting and will not last. These are very accurate assumptions in the world of content. Focusing on content makes everything deteriorate. The more you own, the more there is for you to maintain. Consequently, the more you must protect and defend what you own. The more you think your opinions and judgments must be true, the more time and energy you must put into the defense of them.

Process is not fleeting; it is ongoing. Focusing on process guarantees that there will be no degeneration; instead there will be curiosity and vitality. The more you know (content), the less you grow (process). When we are attempting to maintain content, we must continually assess the condition and degree of decay or strength of the content. As physics teaches us, it is not possible to know the speed and location of any particle at any point in time. It is impossible for you to know where you are and where you're going at the same time. Thus, time spent assessing either where you are or where you are going takes you away from the other. Consciousness constantly wants to know both where it is and where it is going, and since this is impossible, consciousness keeps very busy grasping at any illusion of security.

What is necessary to be alive? Not much. Probably only air, water, food and light. Anything beyond these necessities is a luxury. What would life be like if you were satisfied any time the elements of necessity were met? You would be satisfied a lot. There is a biological link between you and the four necessary elements: air, water, food and light. There is no biological link between you and a new car, you and your opinions, you and money, or you and your career. There is a certain honesty to the biological link which is a fact of life. To pretend that there are other necessities that have a biological link to life is dishonest. The more honest you are in this regard, the more you can live in harmony with yourself, watching as the outside world reflects that harmony. Harmony is knowing your connection with what is; dissonance is acting as if you are not connected and thinking your consciousness is reality. Dissonance is anti-biological; harmony is biological. It is possible to own a lot of things and not be oppressed by the content. It is also possible to own nothing and spend life focusing on what you don't have. Content, by itself, is not a problem. The problem begins when consciousness confuses content with self and no longer distinguishes between the two.

You will live exactly as long as you live. The length of your life at the level of process is not in question. The quality of your life is very much in question. Quality of life is determined by the use and perception of consciousness. You have determined your present quality of life almost entirely without knowing it. By practicing Cognitive Harmony, you can influence the quality of the rest of your life consciously. This endeavor may be cumbersome at first, so keep in mind that anything worth doing is worth doing poorly at first.

Since the stream of life is in a constant flow, it takes a lot of effort and energy to have it appear as though it is not moving. You must either run along with the flow to give it the illusion that it is not flowing or disregard all evidence that it is flowing while reinforcing all evidence that it is stationary. This is a difficult illusion to maintain, and it takes all of your conscious awareness to sustain it.

If you meet someone who lives and talks as though it were still the 1920's, you would probably think he was strange. That is what you are doing by maintaining a consistency of judgments and opinions. The difference is that, unlike the person living in the past, you have agreement and support for your consistency from the people who have perspectives similar to your own. Observations, judgments and opinions must be updated every moment or they separate from what is and attach to what was.

Time can motivate you to act now or allow you to miss the present while focusing on the past or future. You created time, so you can now use it wisely or foolishly. Quantity is a factor in the illusion of time. Quality is the result of attending to the reality of the present. There can never be a problem in the present; there can only be a problem when the past or the future becomes our primary focus. The easiest way to live in the present is to notice the physical sensations you are having right now. When you miss the present, the past and future creep in by having you build expectations, wants and illusions that do not coincide with reality. These expectations, wants and illusions separate consciousness from reality, creating dichotomies which are the root of problems. If you entertain these illusions thoroughly enough, you will be called crazy. If you only occasionally maintain these illusions, you will have problems every time you notice external data inconsistent with your personal illusion or bump up against reality or other people's illusions. If you live your life without illusion, you will be able to live in the world reacting and responding to stimuli moment-to-moment and behaving appropriately as you embrace reality.

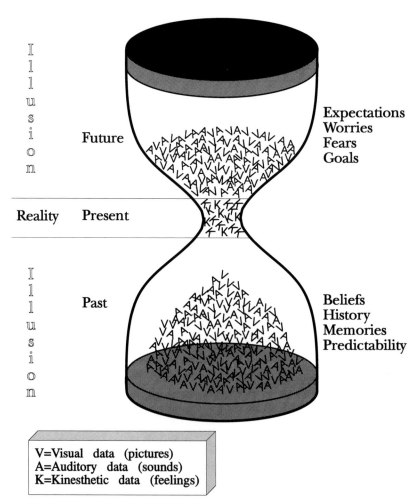

Illustration: Time
Relationship of Past/Present/Future

Time

- Decide that you will live for one more week. What will you do with your week?

- Decide that you will live for one more year. What will you do with your year?

- Decide that you will live for twenty years. What will you do with your twenty years?

- Decide that you will live forever. What would you do with your life if you knew that you would be here forever?

- Decide that you don't know how long you will live. What will you do with that uncertainty?

Think about where you were, how you were thinking and how you were doing five years ago. Take a little time now to reflect back over pictures, sounds and feelings of yourself five years ago. . . . What was some of the content of your life at that time? . . . Notice both grounded and ungrounded assessments. . . . What were your processes five years ago?

Notice where you are now, how you are thinking and how you are doing now. . . . Take a little time to reflect on your pictures, sounds and feelings now. . . . What is your content now? . . . Notice both grounded and ungrounded assessments. . . . What are your processes now?

Notice where you may be in five years, how you may be thinking and how you may be doing. . . . Take a little time to reflect on your pictures, sounds and feelings of five years from now. . . . What might your content be then? Notice both grounded and ungrounded assessments. . . . What might your processes be five years from now?

Labeling

What type of bird has a clearly visible white quarter inch square on both sides of its tail when it flies?

When we label something, our observation tends to shift from that which we are labeling to the label itself. Look closely at the next robin you see as though you do not know what type of bird it is, and you will probably notice the white squares.

Pretend that you have just arrived here from another planet and do not know anything about the earth. Explore the world from this viewpoint with curiosity and without labels. Make new sense of your world. Continually make new sense of your world by interrupting the labeling process. Use your senses to see, hear and feel what is here, not the labels you have applied to what was here.

Practice making new interpretations and investigations of things and events that have become familiar to you. . . . Discover several new things about where you live today. . . . Take a new route to a familiar place today. . . . Take the same route to a familiar place today, but change the focus of consciousness so the route appears different.

Everything in the world is in the process of continually changing. Consciousness wants everything to stay the same. If you think things are the same, alter your focus of consciousness and everything will become different. Move it back, if you can, and everything becomes the same again. You cannot step in the same stream twice but you can think that you have. The stream changes, and to keep up with the stream, you must change your thinking. To change your thinking, learn to change your conscious focus. To learn how to change your conscious focus, practice all the exercises in this book.

15

The Beginning

In the ability to influence our disposition, we are all created equally.

The room doesn't care what you believe; it doesn't care about you or the quality of your life. Quality of life is beyond the power of the room and is left to you.

$\mathcal{Y}$our perceptions are constantly changing. Perceptions are based on the information that you are presented and the types of file searches that are inspired in you. Judgments, opinions and beliefs are constructs of consciousness, manufactured in an attempt to lend meaning and stability to your perceptions. To confuse your constructs of consciousness with perceptions or your perceptions with the world is to mistake metaphor for reality. Wherever your conscious constructs and your perceptions overlap, there is madness. Madness is the continued existence of a person without the continued connection of that person to reality. Consciousness wants stability at any cost. The world is seldom predictable and when this fact becomes apparent, consciousness will ignore variations and fabricate similarities so they look predictable to you. The initial cost of this fabrication of reality is accuracy.

Expectations

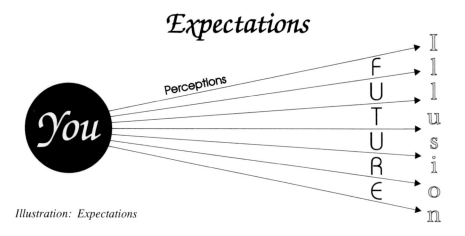

Illustration: Expectations

Observations

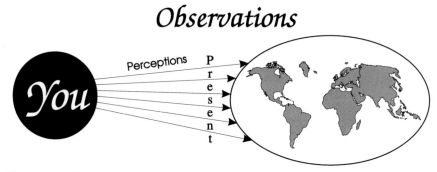

Illustration: Observations

Beliefs

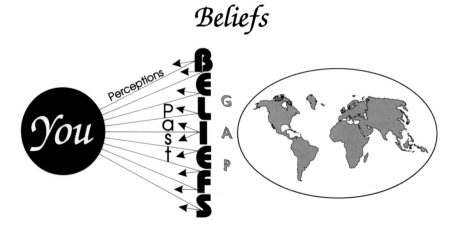

Illustration: The Gap Created by Beliefs

To argue for judgments, opinions and beliefs is to argue for stability in an ever-changing world. It may appear that you are winning an argument or two with this approach, but you are doomed to lose because rigidity in an ever-changing world is not maintainable, survivable or even biologically rooted. Arguments demand tying life, which is by definition even less stable than non-life, to the illusion of stability. This illusion inflicts partial states of death on life, yet even death is more vital and changing than is consciousness when it is continually creating repetitive focus for stability's sake. Stability of conscious focus results in your using an inordinate amount of energy on the constructs of consciousness and moving away from reality. Beliefs are the final stage in this stability of conscious focus. A belief commands conscious rigidity beyond the scope of reasoning. Faith, on the other hand, requires surrendering to what is. Faith involves trust, respect, and surrender. A belief attempts to predict future perceptions based on present rigidity and lack of flexibility. Faith accepts and creates all present perceptions exactly as they are and all future perceptions exactly as they will be.

As far as I can tell, if you believe that "the cat is on the mat," it is unlikely that the cat or the mat care one way or the other about your belief. It is even unlikely that your belief will influence to a significant degree either where the cat or the mat are or the relationship between them. You can only have a significant influence on your perception of the cat, the mat and the way they relate by being in the presence of both the cat and the mat without preconceptions or prejudice. If you believe the cat is on the mat, it is likely that you will see the cat on the mat whether it is there or not. Beliefs are very influential. They prejudice the types of distinctions we are able to make with our senses at a fundamental level. We use judgments to create our reality and then claim that there is an external reality that we have somehow perceived accurately. Beliefs influence perceptions to such a degree primarily because they are impervious to counter examples. Counter examples have a way of allowing consciousness to continually correct and calibrate itself. When we do not see what is around us because we believe it simply couldn't be there, then rigidity has temporarily won and is setting up an illusionary reality which will soon collide with reality. Each new collision with reality is larger and less enjoyable than the last one.

It is not possible to discuss what is actually real in any given situation. However, it is possible to discuss what one is able to perceive, while remembering that perceptions are influenced, at their very roots, by beliefs. Just keeping this in mind is fruitful and releases you from much of life's rigidity, but it requires constant attention and rigor.

Webster's dictionary defines belief as an acceptance of something as true. This is contrary to my explanation above in that most people believe that at some level they can actually determine what is true, forgetting that they are determining what they perceive as true by the beliefs they are holding at the time. A belief rapidly becomes a problem since there are discrepancies between what is actually true (which we may never know) and what we perceive as true. When you are operating on inaccurate information, you may get into trouble. The trouble occurs as you get further and further away from what is actually true while thinking that you are still perceiving the truth. Being removed from the truth in this way is a sin, by which I mean off the mark. Being off the mark is not bad in itself; however, it becomes problematic when you are off-target and believe you are on the mark. Self-correction of perception becomes impossible when perception is created by belief.

If, as a primitive hunter, you are certain that you have hit a deer with an arrow when in fact you did not hit it, you may behave inappropriately. You may follow the deer until it dies of natural causes still certain that you caused its death. With a well-rooted belief, you would be able to ignore the lack of evidence for your arrow's accuracy and even disregard your own hunger and well-being in your pursuit of the unwounded deer. You would lose your own path in life and become an imitation and shadow of the hunted animal. The hunt now becomes your only game, more important than having food. And to keep playing you must forget it is a game. The quality of your life is overshadowed by a pursuit of what is not.

Observing ourselves provides us with a real measure of how off the mark or on-target we are. The closer our perceptions are to what is actually true, the more accurate and less out of touch we are with the present. The smaller the gap is between beliefs and perceptions, the less likely it is you will fall into the gap and be consumed. When you are outside of the gap, you can experience the qualities of life yourself; when you're inside it, you must hold on for dear life to any illusion created by consciousness. When you live outside the gap between beliefs and perceptions, you can walk in the world and simply "be"; when you live inside the gap, you must continually create and defend what you believe the world to be and compulsively "do." You become a "human-doing" instead of a "human-being."

It is likely that a bus will hit you whether you believe the bus is there or not. It is easy and painless for you to act as if the bus is there when it is there. The closer to reality you get, the easier and more natural your life becomes. A word of warning is necessary here: **PICK YOUR BELIEFS CARE-FULLY**. Don't pick them on the basis of whether or not you think they are true. Pick your beliefs by considering the types of behaviors and perceptions that will result from them. Determine whether those behaviors and perceptions make your life easier and lighter or harder and gloomier.

Beliefs are a seldom-explored area. They are so easy to look at from outside their realm and so difficult to notice when you are under their influence. We tend to so thoroughly identify our beliefs as who we are that to examine them, we must begin by discovering ourselves independent of beliefs, which is a difficult task. It is like starting over from the beginning in each moment.

It is unlikely that you would plan a trip into space without taking oxygen along or that you would plan a long voyage without making plans as to where you will stay and what you will eat. Think of the last time you packed for a long trip or the last time you moved. You may have been surprised by the quantity of things you owned or wanted to take along. It is more likely that you would move or go on a long trip without taking anything along than that you would walk around even for a few minutes, without your beliefs. You might not even recognize what you call "yourself" without your beliefs. Over time, as you continue to question and explore beliefs, you will discover that who you really are is a self, independent of beliefs and the illusion of security that beliefs allow. You may recognize yourself as someone who represents a new beginning and limitless possibilities each moment. You will discover yourself beyond the present limitations of consciousness that have made you currently unable to imagine yourself beyond consciousness.

Beliefs come about by habituating one file search while you face the bombardment of stimuli from the outside. Beliefs are an argument that one file search is the right one and all other file searches are less right or even wrong. The more we repeat and habituate a search, the more likely it is that our future will be dominated by the persistence of that specific search of our files. Beliefs and perceptions are mutually exclusive. Life is the process of consistently perceiving in the present. Beliefs are consistently limiting perceptions by replacing them with stored data from your files. Perceptions are not predictable. To be vital, alive and living in the present, you must be ready for whatever comes along. To survive, you must only maintain your base level of biological functioning.

Putting together "causes and effects" is a tactic often used to justify beliefs in their initial stages. When you create a "cause and effect," you are claiming that there is a true, dependent and consistent relationship between things; a relationship that you are able to perceive which then allows you to predict the future. Given our limited focus of consciousness and the ever-changing nature of life, assigning effects to causes can never be true, consistent and predictable. Cause and effects, if held closely enough, can influence what you are able to think and perceive; and lead to the construction of beliefs. Creating "cause and effects" leads you away from perceiving the present as you attempt to predict the future based on your knowledge. It also contributes to the act of building a belief, which is a conscious attempt to predict the future based on habit. Consciousness makes the ungrounded assessment that it is safe if it can predict the future. Gambling, sporting events, and lotteries are attempts to entertain ourselves by predicting the future. If we are right, we win money. If we are not, we lose. Gamblers have their systems for determining the future, and it is the possibility of loss that powers the system. How many gamblers would continue to gamble if they always won? Not many; gamblers feed on the reality of losing and the possibility of winning while missing the ecstasy of now.

Consciousness is a gambler. Consciousness must determine what is going to happen next and avoid uncertainty at the cost of reality. As a friend of mine says, "Often wrong, but never in doubt." The stakes are high for the gambles of consciousness. The stake is life: since life is only available for living in the present, which is a place consciousness rarely goes. The gambler can choose to sit out a hand or a game; consciousness cannot.

Pictures, sounds and feelings are more elementary building blocks than are opinions, judgments, "causes and effects" or beliefs. By playing with the basic building blocks, you can supervise construction. You can make sure that the foundation is secure and well grounded. It is easier to build on earth than in space. Disregard for pictures, sounds and feelings jeopardizes your construction. Since you are always under construction (or in process), it is easier to build from nothing than from the partial ruins of past opinions, judgments and beliefs. If you think these partial ruins are a beautiful tribute to yourself, there will be little room for quality of life to move in. Your life can be a museum of old relics, a temple for reality or a cloud of floating could be's. But regardless of your blueprints, it is most effective to begin building from nothing.

It is not possible to discover who you are or what you are able to be if you cannot separate yourself from your beliefs. This is a tender subject since consciousness often operates as if *who we are* is the same as *what we believe*.

Who you really are is up to you; it is always up to you. Once when I was having a difficult time I said, "All I need is to see the light at the end of the tunnel and everything will be better." A friend of mine overheard me and said that if I had to wait for the light at the end of the tunnel, I was in trouble because there may not be a light. At that moment I realized that at each and every moment, I had to consciously determine the quality of my life. Otherwise I could continue to lie about it and claim that I had to wait for circumstances to determine my life.

This same friend of mine was never very interested in circumstances. He flunked out of college, got upset, and very quickly explored what to do next. Over the next several months he wrote a forty page paper on why he should be admitted to one of the top universities in the country on full scholarship. He loved writing the paper and submitted it to the university when it was finished. Within the year he was enrolled at his chosen university on a full ride scholarship. He did not have the credentials or the money to attend this university, but he did have the will and alternatives to make it happen. He graduated near the top of his class, completing his schooling at the university with the same flair, curiosity and drive he had used to write the forty page paper. I don't know what he is doing now, but I am sure he is not waiting for the light at the end of the tunnel.

This book is about life, as you are about life. Your life is your only resource: it is all you have and all you can ever have. There are a lot of illusions around to keep you busy while you are spending life. And you are spending life, in each and every moment. What are you spending it on? Are you spending it in joy and ecstasy, or getting by and looking good, or defending yourself and complaining? Are you more interested in being right or simply being? You cannot have both.

What aren't you afraid of?

Viewed as a process, life holds only one threat. It is the threat of missing life by being unaware and by never noticing that your life is only yours to live. There is nowhere to get to, so there is no possibility of not getting there. Since there is nothing special to do, each new moment can and will be different. Your life consists of your perceptions, conscious focus and disposition. As you live in the present, the past and future disappear as negative influences. You become able to notice your perceptions and influence your conscious focus and disposition. You become flexible enough to live in an ever-changing world. You return to the flow of life and live it with personal ease. Life becomes an adventure, your adventure.

What are you afraid of?

The motivation behind most human behavior after age six is fear. That may sound like a radical statement and there are exceptions, but they are few and far between. Up until about age six, the main driving force is curiosity and exploration. We learn most of the necessary behaviors, skills and actions which contribute to our development and perpetuation of consciousness between birth and six years of age. We expect learning and flexibility in a young child. We expect knowledge and rigidity from an old person. This is silly. This isn't life; this is the final triumph of the least fit. This is a cultural joke.

What would happen if, as you grow older, you learn to ask more perceptive questions? ... you increase the range of what you can learn?... and you become more and more flexible each day?

Somewhere around six years of age we start paying attention to how we look and whether we are right. We begin to neglect our drive to discover what we can learn and focus on what we already know. We begin to shrink to fit the limitations of adulthood. We begin waiting for the quality of life to happen to us and hope we will be ready if and when it does. We tie our hopes to certain occupations, events, things or people. Tying our hopes this way restricts our movement and limits our continued expansion. How we appear or might appear to others becomes the driving force behind our behaviors and actions while the fear of looking bad starts to influence our choices. We care more about how we look than how we are. Appearance becomes paramount and reality becomes secondary. Content becomes the proving ground for how we look, and we are willing to sacrifice everything for the content of our judgments and opinions. We spend our time wondering what the consequences of a behavior are and how we will look before, during and after the behavior. What other people will think of us becomes more important than being curious about the behavior itself. Our peers help us in this transition by judging our behaviors harshly, making fun of us if we don't behave in the "right" way and by becoming self-conscious themselves. This newfound self-consciousness, which has nothing to do with consciousness focused on self, and fear of doing something wrong slows down the learning process tremendously. We begin the process that we will perfect later, that of assessing all of our behaviors as to their acceptability by whatever standards have been effectively enforced upon us.

When you were four and someone invited you to the park to play, you either went to the park or you didn't. As an adult you ask yourself questions like these: What does he really mean by inviting me to the park? What does he really want? What kind of play? What is he hiding? What else could I get done if I did not go to the park? Is going to the park really the best use of my time? Did I enjoy my last trip to the park? Will he ever invite me to the park again if I don't go this time? Will he perceive my not going as rejection? Will he perceive my going as encouragement? Will there be other people at the park? What should I wear to the park? What is he wearing? — It is little wonder that as we age, and learn to slaughter opportunities with our auditory track, that life loses spontaneity! The more rigid we are and the more we attempt to do what we should, the less spontaneity and flexibility we exhibit.

Given this thinking-to-excess orientation, we learn quickly to tame our curiosity and make sure that we say and do the right thing in any given situation. In other words, instead of exploring our environment, we are the victims of our environment. We lose the ability to dictate our own conscious focus and attempt to prove our conscious control over life. We do the minimum and we make sure that the minimum is expected of us, and we become automated sleepwalkers in the pursuit of safety at the cost of life. We sell our autonomy for fear reduction so that by our early teens, we are so used to living with fear as our primary motivation that we even forget that there are other alternatives.

In a life motivated by fear reduction, the most important thing to remember is never to make a mistake or an error. If, heaven forbid, we do make an error, we must correct the error as soon as possible. Look around you at all of the things that can go wrong. (Remember from Chapter 4, that "wrong" is a matter of interpretation and is an ungrounded assessment based on expectation which arises from a belief.) There are a lot of things that could go wrong; and if only a small percentage of what can go wrong does go wrong, you must spend most of your time in error-correction. And you do. Error-correction is a full-time job and is the principle purpose in life for most people who are involved in fear reduction.

The moment you remember that your worth and safety as a person are based on ungrounded assessments, you open the door to new possibilities. If quality of life is dependent on you, it is your responsibility (ability to respond) to generate and create a quality life. You abandon attempting to look good or do the right thing and you return to the exploration and curiosity that is your nature. Error-correction becomes meaningless because there are no errors. The cessation of error-correction frees up your time and energy and allows you to get on with life. You no longer attempt to make your surroundings predictable by doing the same file searches over and over. Your file searches become as unpredictable as your perceptions, and you experience life while living. You stop waiting and start acting. When you bring satisfaction to life, you no longer have to look for it. You begin to enjoy the process of life. When invited to go to the park to play, you either go or you don't.

Adventure

Whale Tale (Tail)

When I was in the San Juan Islands, I decided that it would be exciting to see the islands from a boat. I met a local person who lent me a small boat for my exploration. The boat was old and very used. He showed me how to take the cover off the motor and make the necessary adjustments to start it. I had neither a map nor much of an idea as to where I wanted to go. I decided that I would travel to another town and have lunch. I had a picture in my head of a short and delightful time traveling around part of the island and enjoying a relaxing lunch. I was to prove myself right only about the delightful time.

I scouted as I went, watching seals, bald eagles and some of the most beautiful coastline I had ever seen. I explored to the sound of the small motor doing its best and the gulls crying overhead, the feeling of the sun warming my back and the smell of salt water in my nostrils. After several hours I began to expect the town to be around every twist and turn of the shoreline. With the optimism of a Midwestern land dweller, I just knew that lunch would come soon and that I couldn't be far from my destination. I didn't realize that I had chosen the long way to get to the next town. The island went on for miles. At one point, I rounded a bend that ended the east side of my boating adventure. I was surprised to discover that the wind was out of the west and that the east side of the island had been protected from the wind and waves. Suddenly, I met waves that were about twice the size of the boat. Undaunted and still optimistic, I continued through the waves following every little bay or inlet, sure that the next bend would harbor the town I had set out for hours before.

Lunch became less and less important as I thought about how long I had been journeying on the same tank of gas. As the gas tank registered half full, I realized I could no longer return the way I had come. The town ahead became even more important for refueling than it was for food. The island continued to be beautiful, but my conversations about the necessity for gas were limiting my ability to see and feel my surroundings.

As the tank approached empty, I realized that I did not want to run out of gas several hundred yards from shore in these waves. I had learned a lesson about the ocean the hard way earlier, by landing the boat on the shore of a small bay to watch some seals. After I had explored the rocky shores and returned to the boat, it was about fifteen feet from the water. The tide was going out and had left the boat far behind. In my Midwest lakes this never happened, nor did I ever have to pull and push a boat over fifteen feet of dry ground to earn the right to float again. My journey would have temporarily ended until the tide came back in if my borrowed boat had been any bigger.

Realizing how fickle the tide is and not knowing whether the tide was all the way out yet, I surveyed the shoreline. I found a pole on shore and tied the boat to it loosely enough so that it could move up or down depending on the movement of the tide. After some walking, I found a gravel road, hiked for several miles and then came upon a paved road. For the first time, I was glad the gas tank was empty as I mused about the difficulties of walking this distance with a full tank to carry. While pondering this, I heard a car. I waved the driver down, asked her where I was and how to get to town. She gave me a ride to town and a ride back to within several hundred yards of the boat. I don't know why I did not look at a map while I was in town or why I did not eat anything. There are no reasons I can come up with to justify that much stupidity in such a short time.

I thanked my chauffeur and headed down toward my boat with the full gas tank. The tide had come back in, so there was no need to drag the boat over dry land this time. Have you ever swum in Puget Sound or any really cold water on a nice windy May day? After a short and chilly swim to the boat and an attempt to dry out, I was on my way in the little boat once again. The question now was whether I should go back the way I had come or continue onward hoping to reach the ocean-side town for dinner or perhaps breakfast the next day. On I went, with a full tank of gas, a smile on my face and an empty stomach. The waves increased in size to what seemed threatening, and amidst the waves I noticed something that splashed above the surface. Then I saw another splash on the other side of the boat. For the next half hour, I was treated to the view and companionship of about thirty killer whales. They jumped, they dove and they sprayed water within thirty feet of my small boat. I had seen whales on television but had never been a witness to their displays before. The boat was smaller than the whales and I was in their element. They came close enough to see me, but did not invite me in for a swim.

Hours later, after going in and out of every curve and bend of the shoreline, I arrived at the town I had set out for. The dinner hour was over and the boat needed more gas. I filled it with gas and bought some crackers and soda and resumed my trip back to where I had started. It was getting dark now but I was back on the east side of the island again, with a full tank of gas and food in my stomach. Several hundred yards from shore and moving along as fast as the boat would carry me, I thought back over my adventure. The excitement of my experience with the whales was still coursing through my body, and the stories I would have to tell about my trip were running through my head. I was as comfortable as I could be after such a day and I knew I would be back at my hotel soon. At this moment I wasn't thinking about the possibility of having the boat meet a rock just under the surface of the water several hundred yards from shore. Nonetheless, the front of the boat launched upward into the air, soon to be followed by the rest of the boat. I did not know that I had made a nick in the propeller because I was too busy bailing the water that was coming in through a small hole in the bottom. Two hours of bailing helped to pass the time between hitting the rock and arriving at the harbor where I had begun my journey.

The boat owner listened to my story with glee and said he could easily fix the hole in the bottom of the boat. I bought him a new propeller to replace the one that hit the rock. This was not the end of my adventure, however; indeed the adventure continues to this day. If you bring adventure with you, it will be wherever you are. Life will be an adventure.

·   ·   ·   ·

As you think back over your life, you will discover that what has happened to you is a "So what!"

Everything you "go-for" is a "So What!" Some people wouldn't dream of becoming President of the United States, but to the people who have been President, it's a "So What!"

Some people wouldn't even dream of becoming a movie star or a millionaire, but to the movie stars and millionaires it is a "So What!"

Everything that you do is a "So What!", unless you add the "So ...!"

It is you with your ungrounded assessments who adds the value to your own life and to everything you do. If you don't add it, it's not there. If you do add it, no one can take it away from you and no one can influence it. Nobody determines the value and importance of your life unless you make an ungrounded assessment that they do.

Your life is yours to assess as you please and it is you that assesses whether or not you are pleased, satisfied, happy, rich, enlightened or angry.

You are the boss. And the more you know that, the less you will abuse your power to cause yourself trauma by making negative ungrounded assessments. If you are walking amidst wildflowers, you can appreciate the smell of the flowers, the beautiful appearance of the flowers or the sound of the wind blowing through them. You could just as easily complain that the smell is not as strong as it was last year or that your nose isn't working like it used to. You could complain that some of the wildflowers are old and wilted or that you wish it was a calm day and that the breeze would please stop mussing your hair. You don't have much choice about the existence of the flowers, but you have all the choice in the world about your interpretation of and amount of pleasure you derive from the flowers—that's your choice.

As a young child everything was a source of wonder and curiosity for you. You saw and experienced each wildflower newly. But somewhere in life you traded that ability for looking good or being right. You traded curiosity and wonder at the process of life for the "right" content of life. When you were a child it was natural to have that ability. It is natural as an adult also, but often forgotten and neglected.

I wonder how soon you will return to that joyful innocence, full of life and able to enjoy each moment as if it were your first.

I hope this book contributes in some way to your return to the natural ease and mental fitness that are yours.

If you think back on memorable moments (or adventures) of your life, you will notice the pictures, sounds and feelings that were going on at that time. By memorable moments, I mean the times when you were alive, awake and alert—moments when you were friends with life. I think you will discover that in those moments you were not safe. You were at risk and uncertain of the outcome. You were probably living in the moment and using every ability you had as if life mattered. It is possible to have this type of experience climbing a huge mountain, having a baby, flying an airplane for the first time, finishing your first marathon or in any number of experiences. It is also possible to have it every waking moment of every day. You never know what will happen next, so I invite you to bring all of the flexibility, alternatives, curiosity and consciousness that you can to each moment.

Exercises

What beliefs are you operating under now?

Make a list of your top ten beliefs. Make the list practically oriented to everyday life and explore beliefs that are specifically yours. Rather than writing down beliefs like, *I believe the world is round*, or *I believe that the sun will rise tomorrow,* choose beliefs that reflect daily on your personal life. For example: *I believe that I will be successful*, or *I believe that people will be nice to me if I am nice to them.* As you determine your top ten beliefs, keep in mind that your beliefs may not always begin with the phrase, "I believe." You may just say, *I know that I will get a headache if I don't eat by 8:00*, or *I am sure that eating sugar causes cavities.* Prioritize your list by putting your most important belief at the top of the list. The higher a belief is on your prioritized list, the more of your perceptions it will influence and the more it will provide an illusion of security. The higher a belief is on the list, the more you will expand and increase your curiosity and flexibility if you temporarily set it to the side. Go to the next paragraph after you have completed your list. Take whatever time is necessary.

Look over your list of your top ten beliefs. Ask yourself whether these are beliefs that you want to have. Pick one of the beliefs and consider what repercussions result from it (in the area of perceptions and behaviors). Think about where and how you apply this belief. For example, if you believe that, *People will be nice to you if you are nice to them,* then this will probably result in your being nice to people a lot of the time. If you are nice to someone and she is not nice back to you, you will either ignore her or get angry with her. You will develop a whole group of expectations based on this belief and you will apply these expectations to your interactions with people. By expectation, I mean that you will construct ideas of how people will behave that may or may not correlate with how they actually behave. If they are accurate, you will maintain equilibrium. If they are inaccurate, you will probably get upset and have problems. As problems occur, rather than looking to the belief, you will probably blame the other person for not behaving the way she "should" have. Thus, out of belief you have developed expectations that then result in rules for how things should be. These rules allow you to judge your behaviors and other people's behaviors; this process obligates you to be the rule-maker, judge and jury of everything simply by perceiving life through your belief. The cost of unexamined beliefs is high. You become the ruler of the world without the authority to rule. The major problem with this is that other people have different beliefs from yours and they are rulers of the world, too. Thus, unexamined beliefs result in a preponderance of judgmental world rulers and very little room for communication or compassion.

•   •   •   •

In closing, my suggestion to you is to go out and play. That's right. Just go out and play. If you have not done the exercises in the book, do them. If you have done the exercises, you have already discovered that they work. You are already seeing, hearing and feeling results in your life.

Congratulations on reading the book and completing the exercises. Now you get to explore just how good you are willing to have your life be. Surround yourself with people who already have great lives and learn how to make yours even better.

My grandmother lived to be ninety-seven. During the last few years of her life, she acquired the ability to be perpetually in the present without a conscious ability to remember her past or think about the future. She was left with only her disposition toward what she was doing at the moment and her awareness of the present. Her disposition was created newly by her every moment—not past-based or future-based. In fact, her disposition was based on nothing at all. Thus, no movie she ever saw, no conversation she ever had or anything she ever did made any difference to her disposition. What made a difference to my grandmother's last few years was how her disposition had been throughout her life. My grandmother's disposition remained one of compassion, curiosity, awe and wonder at the miraculous nature of life and the joyful gift that being alive is.

It doesn't matter what you do or who you know or how many things you own. To discover what has lasting influence, ask the questions, "Have you made your life worth living?" "Have you enjoyed yourself where you were and in what you were doing when you were there?" In the case of my grandmother, the answer is a resounding—Yes. She discovered early in life that she was the creator of her disposition and that her disposition produced the quality of her life.

How is your disposition? By doing the exercises in this book you can learn to control and influence your disposition, you can learn to live each moment as if it is important and you can enter each new situation with curiosity and satisfaction. This is what I mean by living Cognitive Harmony and playing the game of life. Would you like to play?

For information on discounts and quantity purchases of this book and for information on other books and tapes published by Moose Ear Press, contact:

Moose Ear Press
P.O. Box 335, Chetek, WI 54728
(715) 924-4906

To find out more about *Cognitive Harmony* or for information about seminars lead by Jerry or Jackie Stocking, please contact A Choice Experience. A Choice Experience is a non-profit corporation dedicated to *Cognitive Harmony*.

A Choice Experience
P.O. Box 335, Chetek, WI 54728
(715) 924-4906